HISTORY OF THE
U.S. CAVALRY

HISTORY OF THE
U.S. CAVALRY

SWAFFORD JOHNSON

CRESCENT

A BISON BOOK

Copyright © 1985 Bison Books Corp.

Published 1985 by
Crescent Books, distributed by
Crown Publishers Inc.

Produced by Bison Books Corp.
17 Sherwood Place
Greenwich, CT 06830, USA

Library of Congress Cataloging in Publication Data

Johnson, Swafford.
    History of the US Cavalry.

    ''A Bison book.''
    1. United States.   Army.   Cavalry – History.
I. Title.   II. Title: History of the United States
Cavalry.
UA30.J64   1985   357'.1'0973   85-5772
ISBN 0-517-460831

ISBN 0-517-460831
h g f e d c b a

Contents

The Horse Soldier Through
The American Revolution

Previous pages: General George Washington reviewing his ragged troops at Valley Forge, Pennsylvania, in the terrible winter of 1777-8.

Opposite, top: In the fourth century AD, fierce Asiatic horsemen, the Huns, swept into Eastern Europe to threaten the Roman Empire.

Opposite, bottom: A Roman coin showing the relief of London by Emperor Constantius Chlorus, the father of Constantine (AD 285-337).

Below: Rameses II and his sons in battle, from the Great Temple at Abu Simbel, Egypt.

The history of the US Cavalry should really start with that day, long before written history began, when an imaginative ancestor saw a familiar animal in a new way. That animal, the horse, was familiar to him because it was part of his food supply – our distant forebears first hunted the horse for its flesh and later took to herding the animals for both food and milk. But on the day in question, our ancestor noticed again that this creature moved a good deal faster than he did. And somehow he conceived the radical notion of climbing onto its back and gaining some of its speed for himself.

So it was that this man actually tried to jump onto the back of a horse – and found very quickly that the animal was less than enthusiastic about the idea. But he persisted, and eventually proved that a human being could ride a horse. We don't know when this happened, of course. The oldest evidence to date of man on horseback is a drawing on a bone chip from about 3000 BC, found in the Euphrates Valley. Presumably, people had been riding horses long before that and had already discovered the advantages provided in tracking other four-footed animals or pulling loads. Over the centuries, the practice spread, and as men chose the strongest and fastest horses to ride and breed, the stock improved.

It was probably not long before it became clear that the horse was useful for more than hunting and transportation – that it could also give one a significant edge in disagreements with one's fellow bipeds. The first 'combat horses' we know about, however, were not carrying mounted warriors; they were used to pull 'war carts' – probably little more than supply wagons, although some soldiers must have occasionally hopped on for a ride to the battlefield. Perhaps the oldest graphic representation of such war carts is on the Sumerian 'Royal Standard of Ur,' dated to about 2700 BC, but these rather bulky wagons, with their solid wheels, are drawn by onagers and asses. During the next thousand years or so, this unwieldy type of chariot evolved into the much lighter, swifter and more maneuverable two-wheeled chariot; its wheels,

moreover, had spokes. This type first appears among the Hurrians of North Syria, but these people may have been influenced by the nomadic, horse-culture Indo-European peoples who came off the steppes of Central Asia and Southern Russia in the years after 2000 BC. In the centuries between 2000 and 1000 BC, various peoples of that era – the Babylonians, the Hyksos, the Mycenaeans, the Egyptians, the Chinese – employed the horse-drawn chariot in warfare.

What remained was for men to combine the two traditions: horseback riding and horses in combat. Today this might seem like an obvious step, but it was not until about 1500 BC that the first mounted warriors began to appear (judging, that is, from artifacts and representations found by archaeologists in the Near East). And it is not until after 1000 BC that the mounted warrior – the true cavalryman, as opposed to individual riders who might swoop down on helpless shepherds or villagers – began to play a significant role alongside the chariot forces in battle. The leaders in this seem to have been the Assyrians, who apparently deserved their reputation as the most martial people of the ancient world. The Assyrian armies employed hundreds of thousands of foot soldiers and thousands of chariots and cavalrymen. The cavalry wore leather boots, and some wore a chain mail; they were armed with either bows or lances.

It is unfortunate that the first organized and effective cavalry force is associated with the brutal Assyrians, but ruthlessness would always characterize one type of mounted warrior – call it 'the Cossack element,' the horseman who exploits his advantage against defenseless civilians. But this is not the tradition from which the US Cavalry evolved. Instead, the US Cavalry identified with what might be called 'the Greek element' – the mounted warrior as an elite if not aristocratic member of the military. This status derived from the particular training and skills involved in fighting from a swift steed; he may or may not have been a man of wealth or leisure to acquire these skills, but his code permitted

using his mounted advantage only against armed enemies.

It was this tradition of the cavalry that led Aristotle to write: 'The earliest form of government after the abolition of kingship was one in which the citizen body was drawn exclusively from the warrior class, first represented by cavalry.' Aristotle also knew that his fourth-century BC contemporary, the Macedonian King Philip II, father of Alexander the Great, formed an elite regiment of noblemen on horseback. These riders became the most successful 'shock forces' of Philip's armies, and later of Alexander's.

Like his father, Alexander used his heavy infantry to fix his opponents, then mounted a decisive cavalry charge on the enemy's flanks to rout him. Indeed, Alexander's use of his mounted troops set the pattern for many of cavalry's classic functions through history – reconnaissance, delaying action, raid and pursuit.

These exploits of the ancients are the more remarkable when we consider that mounted warriors of those days rode bareback, often fighting with both hands and controlling the horse with their legs. The bits they used, however, were much like those of modern times: the one-piece snaffle bit dates from at least 1400 BC. Celts of the third century BC produced the curb bit, a snaffle with a chain or thong that fits along the horse's chin.

The military successes of ancient Rome were initially based almost entirely on infantry; for some time Roman cavalry was weak and poorly trained. But when the Carthaginian general Hannibal swept over the Alps with his horsemen and his elephants, the ensuing Punic Wars provided the Romans with a painful and productive lesson in the use of cavalry. The first phase of this era culminated in 216 BC with a devastating Roman defeat by Hannibal at Cannae. As always, however, the Romans were quick to learn from their enemies; in 202 BC Hannibal was defeated by his own tactics at the battle of Zama. Following this victory, Roman military strategy returned to its traditional dependence on infantry, and the cavalry arm languished. One example of the vulnerability of Roman legions to expert horse fighters came in 53 BC at the battle of Carrhae. The Roman general Crassus had taken 34,000 legionaries into the domain of the Parthians, in south-central Asia. On the plains of their country, the mounted Parthians surrounded the Roman Army, keeping well out of range of the legions' spears and swords, and rode around and around Crassus's troops, pouring a hail of arrows into his helpless infantry, mowing them down in waves where they stood. It was one of the great debacles of history.

By about AD 117 the era of Roman conquest had ended, and the Romans turned to cavalry to patrol and secure the borders of their empire. But as time went on, the barbarian hordes of mounted nomads gathering around the empire became too much for Roman military might. In AD 378 Emperor Valens was routed at Adrianople by Gothic horsemen. After the fall of Rome, the power center of the West moved to the growing Byzantine Empire.

Centered in Constantinople, the Byzantines built their power on cavalry, developing a tactical system that won them victories across much of the ancient world. Byzantine mounts had shoes, saddles and stirrups. The riders were primarily heavy – that is, armored – cavalry, expertly wielding both lances and bows from horseback. To the west, another powerful force arose, also based on cavalry – the Franks. In the eighth century Charlemagne began the process of turning the Franks into expert armored horsemen to resist the depredations of the Vikings. Part and parcel of this military development was the evolution of a new social order called feudalism, as military necessity drove the peasants to bind themselves to local warlords for protection. It happened that the best kind of soldier to send against the Vikings was the mailed horseman. Thus began the long history of the mounted knight.

At the Battle of Hastings in 1066, Norman knights defeated the Anglo-Saxons, one of the great infantry hosts of western Europe. On the battlefield the horse was now supreme, and at the head of the feudal social hierarchy rode the knight. The earliest knightly armor was primarily mail, topped by a metal helmet. As the Middle Ages went on, the knight gradually became encased in heavy plate armor, his head protected by an iron pot with thin slits for eyeholes. As armor became heavier the mobility of the knight grew more restricted. Partly for that reason, all the efforts of knighthood were incapable of stopping the Mongols under Genghis Khan, whose unarmored horsemen swept across Asia and into Europe in the thirteenth century.

The Middle Ages were a time of iron men and walled towns. Both were impervious to the weapons of the day – the sword, the bow, the lance. But the arrogance of the knight and his obsession with the idealized glories of chivalry and the grand charge were not to endure. The flower of French knighthood suffered a crushing defeat at the Battle of Crécy in 1346, its charges mowed down at a distance by the newly developed longbows of the English. By that time the instrument of doom for iron men and walled towns alike – gunpowder – had already appeared. The heaviest armor could not stand up under a cannonball, or even a pistol fired at close range. In 1453 the cannons of the Turks broke down the walls of Constantinople and the city fell. With the onslaught of gunpowder weapons, cavalry declined in the 16th and early 17th centuries. But during the Thirty Years' War of the 17th century appeared the man who later earned the title 'father of modern tactics' – King Gustavus Adolphus of Sweden. His innovation was precise co-ordination of his various divisions with

Top: *The Battle of Hastings (Bayeux Tapestry).*

Above: *The Syrians at the Siege of Jerusalem (1099).*

Below: *The Sultan's Guard sounds the call to war against the infidels (Séances d'Harari, 13th-century Arab manuscript).*

Right: *Christians confront Tartars in this illustration from a mid-16th century manuscript.*

Far right: *The Horsemen of the Four Seals, armed like Saracens with crossbows and swords* (Silos Apocalypse, 1109).

Above: *A medieval miniature illuminating the initial of* Carolus Magnus, *the Frankish Emperor Charlemagne.*

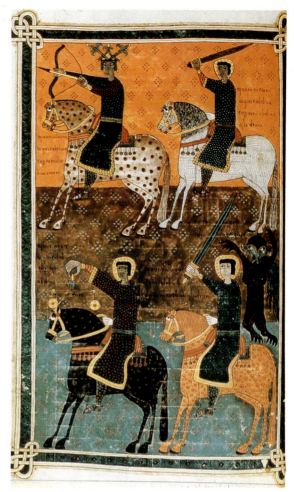

Right: *Horsemen face foot soldiers in the Hundred Years' War, from the 15th-century* Chroniques de Charles VII.

Opposite, top: *Captain Charles May of the US Second Dragoons astonished the enemy at the Battle of Resaca de la Palma by charging Mexican artillery. He and his men gained the time needed for Zachary Taylor's infantry to advance and secure the victory.*

Above: *Charge of the Mexican Lancers at the Battle of Buena Vista.*

Right: *A cavalry recruitment poster for the Mexican War; traditionally, cavalry volunteers furnished their own horses and equipment. One inducement offered here is a 'mileage allowance' of 50 cents per day for use of the horse.*

Mexico and California by whatever means. The means turned out to be war, which Polk incited by sending troops into territory claimed by Mexico. (Texas, meanwhile, had voted itself into the Union.) The Mexican War was never to be a popular one, however; Americans wanted the land, but the means employed left a bad taste in their mouths.

Kearny received a second order from Washington, instructing him to recruit a thousand volunteers from Missouri and a force of Mormons. This was soon done and Kearny was ready to march on Santa Fe. By that time the Second Dragoons were already in the thick of it in Mexico.

General Zachary Taylor – later to be president – was fighting there with his euphemistically named 'Army of Observation'; with him were seven troops of the Second Dragoons. On 8 May Taylor used his infantry and artillery to rout the forces of General Manuel Arista in the Battle of Palo Alto. But General Arista was by no means finished after that day. As the Mexican general moved south with his army, Taylor and his forces followed, catching up with the enemy on the afternoon of 9 May, at Resaca de la Palma. There they found Arista well protected by his artillery, which was positioned to sweep the road on which the Americans were advancing.

Taylor opened up with his own artillery and got his infantry some way forward, but they came to a halt in the face of the Mexican cannon firing from across the shallow ravine of the Resaca. In desperation, Taylor did something that, had he been a West Point man, he would have learned never to do: he called up Dragoon Captain Charles May and told him, 'Charge, Captain! Charge, *nolens volens*.' (It is old military doctrine that cavalry must never charge artillery.) May trotted back to his men, who were waiting in columns of four with their heavy Prussian sabers drawn, and shouted, 'Remember your regiment and follow your officers!' With a snap of his arm he took the Dragoons

forward toward the Mexican artillery.

In short order the troopers were galloping wildly into a storm of canister from the enemy guns; soon a number of saddles were empty. Captain May and a few Dragoons made it over the Mexican breastworks and exercised their sabers. The rest, their horses balking before the breastworks, rode across the enemy line and around to the rear, driving the Mexicans away from their guns. Then they had to force their way back through the enemy artillery position to regain the American lines. The Mexicans quickly reoccupied their cannons, but the charge had given Taylor's infantry time to advance. Arista's Mexicans were routed, the Dragoons hastening them on their way.

All in all, it was a good thing that Zachary Taylor didn't fight by the book at Resaca de la Palma. The gallant charge of the Dragoons had won the day. Soon the Second Dragoons had a new coat of arms, depicting a saber-wielding horseman charging a Mexican cannoneer. In the battle General Arista had nearly 800 casualties; American losses were 39 killed and fewer than 100 wounded.

A month later the First Dragoons were marching down the Santa Fe Trail under Stephen Watts Kearny, moving against Mexican forces in New Mexico. Kearny was soon to be appointed a brevet brigadier general. He and his motley group of Dragoons, Missouri Mounted Volunteers, infantry, artillery, Indian scouts and assorted others – some 1700 in all, with 16 field guns – were ordered to conquer New Mexico. Challenging Kearny's men in the territory was the army of Mexican Governor Manuel Armijo. Kearny drove his column relentlessly, halving rations to save time, sometimes making over 30 miles a day. By early August the rigors of the march were taking their toll; graves began ap-

LINCOLN CAVALRY

Col. ANDREW T. McREYNOLDS, Commanding.

WANTED

A FEW GOOD MEN!

To be in the field by 4th of July, if possible, who can furnish their own horses and equipments.

"EXTRACT FROM OFFICIAL ORDERS."

The allowances for Clothing for Cavalry, shall be $3 50 per month. Each Officer, Non-commissioned Officer, Private, and Musician, shall furnish his own Horse and Horse Equipments. [Equipments and Clothing can be furnished for $50] In case the Horse is lost in action, the Government pays for same 50 Cents a day is allowed for use of Horse.

Some good **FARRIERS** and **BLACKSMITHS**, wanted for the above Regiment, **PAY EXTRA**.

This is the only Cavalry Regiment accepted by the United States Government for immediate Service, and to serve during the War.

☞ Apply immediately to Head Quarters,

403 Walnut Street, Phila.. or to William H. Boyd, Box 661 Post Office.

☞ The person receiving this bill will please post it in a Conspicuous Place

pearing in the wake of the column. By the time they approached Las Vegas the men had marched nearly 1000 miles; at that point the news came that Governor Armijo was waiting for them before Santa Fe with 10,000 men. Undaunted, Kearny hurried on to Las Vegas, ready to fight. Contrary to reports, however, there proved to be no Mexican resistance in the city: Kearny marched in unopposed and raised the flag. Gearing up for action, the column moved on toward the expected battle at Santa Fe. But at the approach of the Americans, Governor Armijo bolted. In reality, he had commanded few troops – most of the Mexican Army was fighting on its own soil in the south. On 18 August Kearny and his column rode peacefully into Santa Fe, raised the flag over the Palace of Governors and declared New Mexico a United States possession. He had conquered a huge territory without firing a shot. Now it was time to move on to the next objective, which would not prove so easy – California.

On 25 September 1846, Kearny and his men set out on the 1000-mile march to California. His five companies of Dragoons were dressed in blue flannel uniforms, each carrying two pistols, a single-shot carbine and a Bowie knife. They had left their sabers at Fort Leavenworth; though Dragoons were still counted in sabers, the age-old weapon of the horse soldier (as opposed to numbers of men), commanders were beginning to realize the limits of the saber's usefulness. Miles behind Kearny rode the newly formed Mormon Battalion, led by Captain Philip

St George Cooke, with orders to follow Kearny and build a wagon road. This time the bulk of Kearny's heterogeneous detachment walked; most of the horses and mules that had died or given out on the way to Santa Fe had not been replaced. All the Dragoons rode mules, many of them already broken down. It was an ominous commencement to a long and frustrating campaign.

However, the first signs were hopeful. On 6 October the column was greeted by mountain man Kit Carson, who brought good news from California: irregulars and US Navy men had taken the territory for the United States and installed as governor the famous explorer John C Frémont, who had become an Army Major. Kearny thought things over, then sent three companies of Dragoons back to Santa Fe. The remaining two companies he placed on the best mounts he had and ordered Carson, who was serving as a temporary lieutenant, to lead the column to California.

The route lay across a fearsome obstacle course of gorges and desert. Of all the difficult marches in US Cavalry history, this one was to prove among the worst. The diary of a participant describes its early stages: 'The only consolation a man has is that his mule is feeding and may be able to carry him another day farther on the journey – our pack animals are getting in a most pitiable condition – their backs are cut all to pieces – and so poor and weak that they can hardly be goaded along.' Water was plentiful enough, as they marched along the Rio Grande

on, sometimes literally pushing their mounts ahead of them and eating mostly horsemeat, bad news arrived from California: Mexican Californians had revolted against US rule, conquered all of California south of San Luis Obispo and installed a Mexican governor in place of Frémont. On 3 December they were at Warner's Ranch, 60 miles from San Diego, nearly 1900 miles from Fort Leavenworth. There they learned the full extent of the counterrevolution – Mexicans controlled the entire state except for San Francisco, San Diego and Monterey.

Kearny requested supplies from American Commodore Stockton in San Diego: none were forthcoming. The Dragoons had managed to secure some remounts intended for the Mexicans, and a few volunteers, Marines and sailors joined the column. Learning on 5 December that a Mexican Army led by General Andres Pico lay nine miles distant, Kearny moved his weary column forward. The very idea of mounting an offensive with his played-out men and mounts was something of an absurdity, but that was what Kearny determined to try. It was what he had marched here for, after all.

In the early morning of 6 December, in a freezing drizzle, Kearny moved to the attack. The Mexicans, having been alerted, were waiting for him in front of the village of San Pasqual, which lay in a narrow valley. All the Americans could do was sweep in one end and hope to drive the enemy out the other. Fifty Dragoons charged into the Mexicans at a gallop; after emptying several American saddles and shooting Kit Carson's horse from under him, the Mexicans scattered back around the valley. For a few moments things seemed to be going well. Then the Americans, smelling victory, made a disorderly advance on into the valley. Their impetuousity invited disaster, and disaster struck on cue. Suddenly the Dragoons found themselves flanked by Mexican lancers, who closed in

Opposite, top: The dressy Dragoon uniform of 1851 had come a long way from the slapdash garb of the Revolutionary War. From left: Colonel, Sergeant Major, Musician.

Above: Kentucky cavalrymen played a distinguished part in the victory of Buena Vista, Mexico, although Scott's infantry forces were far more numerous.

Right: Colonel William S Harney commanded the Second Dragoons at this fight near Medelia, not far from Vera Cruz. Later he served under Philip Kearny at Churubusco, in the final push toward Mexico City.

and then along the Gila River, but food was a continuing problem; their cattle were dying on the trail, local Indians were sometimes willing to sell them food, sometimes not.

In the last week of November, Kearny and his starving, half-naked and exhausted men – and a few animals in similar straits – crossed the Colorado into California. The territory in front of them was, if anything, worse than what they had already crossed – there was little but heat and assorted shades of sand. As the men staggered

and broke apart Kearny's attack in brief and bloody fighting. Americans were lanced and lassoed off their horses to be dispatched on the ground; Kearny was wounded while fencing with an enemy. The American attack repulsed, the Mexican lancers rode away from San Pasqual leaving 19 Americans dead and 15 wounded. Minus mounts and supplies, Kearny and his men limped to the San Bernardo Ranch. San Pasqual had been a most ill-advised and - executed attack, with predictably dismal results. Though only a small skirmish by most wartime standards, it was the bloodiest day of the war in California and a humiliating defeat for the Dragoons.

Kearny's men held on in their camp for days while Pico's forces pressed in on them. Finally, on 11 December, reinforcements arrived from Commodore Stockton. Pico then pulled away, and the Americans trudged on to the Pacific Coast at San Diego, the endpoint of one of the most grueling marches in the nation's history. Perhaps they found some satisfaction in that. They certainly found some in January 1847, when Kearny, recovered from his wound, led combined American forces to defeat the Mexicans at Los Angeles. Once again, and for good, the American flag flew above the city.

This victory was soon followed by General Winfield Scott's successes in Mexico at Buena Vista, Vera Cruz and elsewhere; these were largely infantry affairs. But Scott had noticed the fighting spirit of cavalryman Phil Kearny, Stephen Watts Kearny's young nephew. Phil had raised a crack outfit of his own, the Gray Horse Troop, which became Scott's guard of honor. In August of 1847, Scott was pursuing his campaign against General Santa Anna. The Second Dragoons were commanded by Colonel William S Harney and included the men of Phil Kearny's troop. On 20 August the opposing armies were poised for battle at Churubusco, near Mexico City. Phil Kearny asked Scott for a transfer from headquarters duty to the battle line, and Scott complied.

The armies of Generals Scott and Santa Anna crashed together and the fighting surged back and forth, American infantry and Dragoons pushing into the Mexicans' center and routing them. Kearny and the other horsemen pursued the fleeing enemy infantry with their sabers. When a few Dragoons had gotten ahead of the infantry, Kearny rode forward, pistol in one hand, saber in the other, the reins in his teeth. The Dragoons had advanced so far that Scott ordered a bugler to sound the recall. Kearny later admitted he heard the recall, but added, 'I was sure it was not for me.' He kept advancing, with some dozen Dragoons, until they found themselves dismounted right in front of the Mexican lines. As the Mexicans swarmed around them, the Dragoons formed a circle and fought with sabers; as a man was killed, the one behind used his body for a shield. Finally, a few of them tore away. Phil Kearny leaped on his horse and

40

Insert top left: *An aging General Winfield Scott (nicknamed by his men 'Old Fuss and Feathers') sat for this portrait after the Mexican War.*

Main picture: *The Battle of Vera Cruz, showing the American squadron bombarding the Mexican fortress.*

Above: *Scott's triumphal entry into the Mexican capital in 1847 presaged the acquisition of vast new Western territories, which a comparative handful of US Cavalrymen would have to safeguard and pacify.*

Charles Schreyvogel painted this scene wherein a cavalryman covered by two comrades rescues his bunkmate from attacking Indians.

somehow escaped, but not before enemy grape-shot claimed his left arm. It did not damage his military career, which would continue into the Civil War – Kearny was used to riding with the reins in his teeth.

The Americans won the day at Churubusco, and on 13 September 1847, Winfield Scott led his victorious forces into Mexico City. The Mexicans soon asked for peace. By hook and by crook, President Polk had made good on his vow to secure Texas, New Mexico and California, adding a million square miles to US territory. Though horse soldiers had been in action throughout the war, neither Winfield Scott nor Zachary Taylor had used them in anything approaching their true capacity. American generals simply had not yet discovered the real potential of mounted units. Robert E Lee and Jeb Stuart would teach them that lesson.

After the war with Mexico, Stephen Watts Kearny had only a year to live; most of that year was spent in a bitter wrangle with fractious John C Frémont, who was court-martialed for defying Kearny's orders in California. But Kearny died with a solid accomplishment behind him: more than anyone else, he had built the cavalry into a proud, effective and firmly established branch of the US Army.

In 1849 gold was discovered in California, and the stream of settlers heading west swelled to a flood that would scarcely ever abate. The Dragoons and the army turned their attention to policing the trails and settlements of California, Utah and Oregon. There were continual calls from settlers to suppress – often to annihilate – the Indians. The army had to walk a narrow course between the professedly benevolent attitude of the government toward nominally peaceful Indians and the fearful and hostile attitude of the settlers toward any and all Indians, whose lands the settlers wanted and were getting, piece by piece. It was an impossible situation, a kettle boiling toward eventual violence and tragedy, just as other tensions were simmering toward eruption of the Civil War.

If Stephen Watts Kearny shepherded the Dragoons in their infancy and adolescence, it was his old partner Philip St George Cooke who seasoned them into maturity after Kearny's death. Cooke had been a Dragoon since the Dodge expedition, growing up along with the regiment. After the Mexican War he was named Lieutenant Colonel of the Second Dragoons; in the absence of his superior, Colonel Harney, he was its real commander. Thus Cooke took over the reins of Indian fighting in the West. Though there was never to be an all-out Indian offensive before the Civil War, army statistics of the 1850s record 22 'wars' and 37 'engagements' that saw casualties. It was a nerve-wracking, ever-widening guerrilla warfare that Cooke and his men waged.

In 1855 President Franklin Pierce's secretary of war, Jefferson Davis – who would become president of the Confederacy five years later – decreed four new army regiments, which raised the number of men in arms from 10,000 to 15,000. Two of the new regiments were mounted, but this time they were called not Dragoons but the First and Second Cavalry – the first units so named in the US Army. The reasons for the new designation are hazy: it is quite possible that it had to do with the autocratic Davis, who kept the new outfits separate in command so as to put his favorites at their helms. Among the officers of the cavalry were a number of men destined to be much heard of in the Civil War, most of them on the Confederate side. Commanding the First Cavalry was Edwin V Sumner, later a Union general; his lieutenant colonel was to be one of the great Southern generals, Joseph E Johnston. Officers of the Second Cavalry included such future Confederates as Albert Sidney Johnston, William J Hardee, John B Hood and Lieutenant Colonel Robert E Lee.

The only real differences between the old Dragoons and the new Cavalry were in name and dress; both were essentially light cavalry, as were the divisions called Mounted Rifles. In theory, each kind of outfit carried different weapons; in practice, they carried whatever was handy: old breechloading smoothbore Hall carbines, cavalry musketoons and a few of the new breechloading Sharps carbines. Some troopers also sported Colt six-shooters, replacing the old single-shot horse pistols. Usually left at home was the saber, which was manifestly of little use in fighting Indians. As was often the case, it was the enlisted men who knew better than their officers what worked on the battlefield

Above: *Schreyvogel's dramatic painting* Fight for the Water Hole *gives a sense of the unequal struggle between white man and Indian for possession of the West.*

Left: *Frederic Remington's colorful and authentic portraits of Western Americana include this view of off-duty US Cavalrymen playing cards – *Dispute Over a Deal.

and what didn't; to the end of his career Cooke favored carrying sabers, and army brass refused to consider the repeating carbine until well into the Civil War. It was an era of bewilderingly rapid developments in weaponry, so the inertia of tradition was probably inevitable.

By the 1850s the cavalrymen had fallen into habits of dress as random and makeshift as their weaponry. Their clothes were a heterogeneous collection of official issue of various periods supplemented *ad hoc* by each trooper. A young cavalryman of the 1850s wrote home from the frontier, 'I wish you could see me in my scouting costume. Mounted on my mule [with] corduroy pants; a hickory or blue flannel shirt, cut down in front, studded with pickets and worn outside; a slouched hat and long beard, cavalry boots worn over the pants, knife and revolver belted to the side and a double barrel gun across the pommel, complete the costume, as truly serviceable as it is unmilitary.' After 1847 army horsemen changed from a saddle much like the

modern English to the Grimsley saddle, which was standard until the coming of the McClellan saddle just before the Civil War.

In the West the army tended to use infantry to hold posts, mounted men actually to engage the Indians. In that era such campaigns always proved fairly short and more or less successful, however bloody. There were two non-Indian campaigns of interest just before the war. In 1856 Kansas was about to become a state and was torn by factions for and against its coming in with slaves. Abolitionists were moving their sympathizers into the area and pro-slavery men were raiding from Missouri. It was a volatile situation, emblematic of the pressure that was building all over the country. Jefferson Davis sent Cooke into Kansas to keep the peace and the Dragoons did so – just barely – with an even-handedness that won respect from both factions. Meanwhile, Colonel Sumner and the First Cavalry separated gangs led by fanatic abolitionist John Brown and a Missouri pro-slave hood-

Above: *A realistic interpretation of the Western emigration experience: a view of Devil's Gate Landmark on the Oregon Trail through Central Wyoming.*

Right: *This romanticized pastoral scene, titled* Bedding Down for the Night, *was painted by Benjamin Franklin Reinhart. Few pioneers would have recognized themselves (or their livestock) in this tableau.*

Left: *Painter George Catlin accompanied the Dodge Expedition and suffered many hardships, including a near-fatal illness, in his quest to capture the receding frontier on canvas. This impressive oil of Chief Keokuk, who sought peace with encroaching settlers on behalf of the Saux and Fox tribes, was painted in 1835.*

45

Above: *US Cavalrymen defend their stockade against marauding Indians, in this Schreyvogel painting that epitomizes the mythos of the American West.*

Left: *Many cavalrymen who served on the frontier would bring their hard-won experience into the Civil War, where American Cavalry came into its own. Their uniforms might be either blue or grey, but the saber remained a badge of distinction.*

Right: *Schreyvogel's* The Duel *pits a skilled Plains warrior against a saber-wielding trooper. There was perhaps only one thing for which the native American was truly grateful to the white man — the horse, introduced by the Spanish into the New World.*

Right: *Cavalryman Albert Sidney Johnston commanded the army of the Republic of Texas before he served in the Mexican War. His promising Confederate Army career would be cut short by a mortal wound at Shiloh in 1862.*

Above: *Bactrian camels were imported and tried out as cavalry mounts in the Western desert before the Civil War, but this costly experiment was short-lived.*

Right: *The diverse uniforms of the newly formed Confederate Army in 1861.*

lum; if the two gangs had started shooting, the Civil War might have started then and there. With the Dragoons maintaining the peace, Kansas had calmed down by autumn of 1856, and most of the horse soldiers returned to post-duty and Indian-fighting at Forts Leavenworth and Riley.

The next year saw one of the odder episodes in US Cavalry history. President James Buchanan determined to reassert government sovereignty over the Mormons, who had long had a rocky and ambiguous relationship with Washington, in the Territory of Utah. To Mormons, all others were 'gentiles' without jurisdiction over the Saints. Buchanan sent a detachment of the Second Cavalry under Colonel Albert Sidney Johnston toward Salt Lake City to uphold Federally appointed authorities in Utah. Advised of their coming, Mormon leader Brigham Young vowed defiance: 'Woe, woe to that man who comes here to unlawfully interfere with my affairs. Woe, woe to those men who come here to unlawfully meddle with me and this people.' While the Federal expedition trudged through the Rockies during the winter, Young began to organize an army.

For the horse soldiers it was an awful winter. Cooke and the Dragoons pushed through the mountains trying to catch up with Johnston's infantry detachment. Temperatures fell to 44 degrees below zero Fahrenheit, with vicious winds, blizzards and deep snow. Only ten of nearly 150 Dragoon horses survived the trek. The two detachments finally pulled into Fort Bridger on the road to Salt Lake City, where they rested in a morass of trooper disaffection and command wrangles between Cooke and Johnston. At length they learned that something of a

political settlement had been patched up between the US Governor of Utah and Brigham Young, which let the air out of the conflict and saved face for everyone. However, General Johnston insisted on parading his forces into Salt Lake City. That parade, on 26 June 1857, was a singular spectacle. In order not to countenance this show of US authority, the Mormons had pulled out of the city lock, stock and barrel, leaving nothing but empty buildings to witness Johnston's display. When the cavalry left, the Mormons moved right back in.

Now the Dragoons and Cavalry went back to Indian management for some time. In 1858 there was a short-lived attempt to mount Dragoons on camels; it proved an imaginative but useless experiment. Then, in 1860, the long-simmering tensions between North and South erupted, and the horse soldiers were caught up in the resulting explosion to find their greatest challenge, one that divided them as it divided the nation.

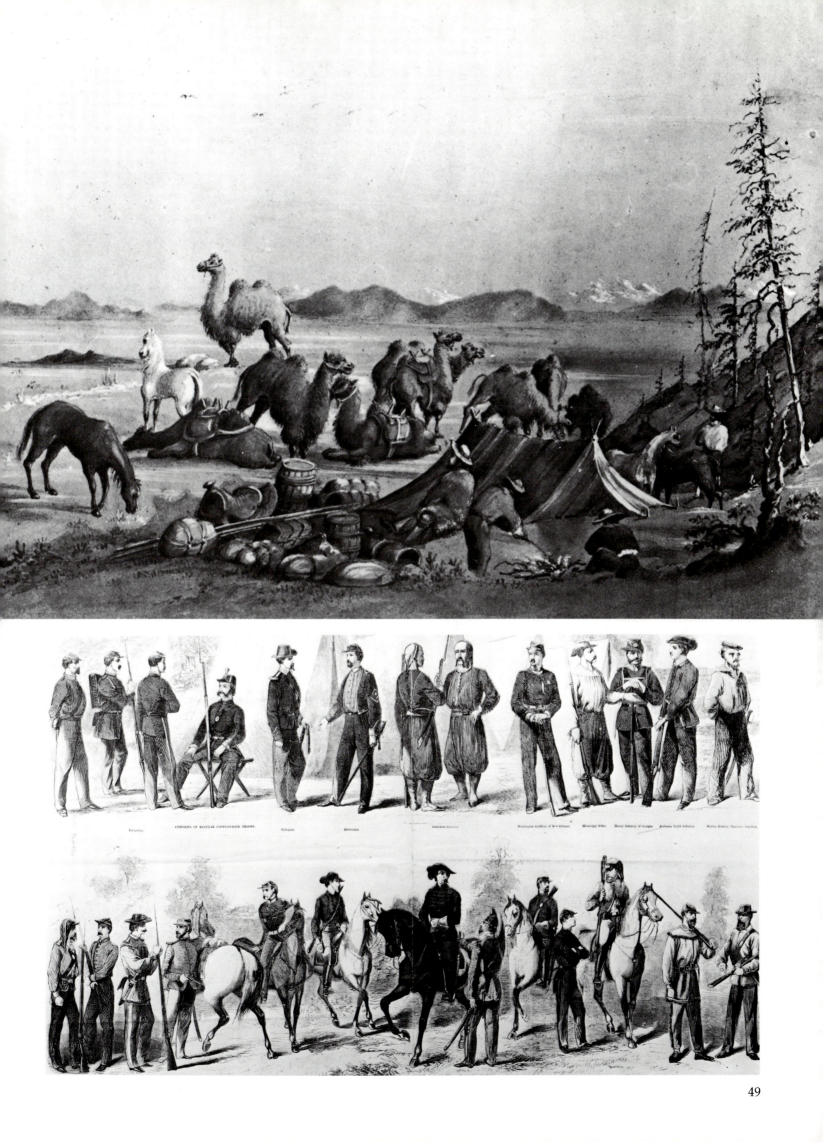

Cavalry at Hanover, Pennsylvania, and charged them; the Federals broke and then re-formed, mounting a counterattack that routed the Confederates in turn. This time the Yankees very nearly bagged a big prize indeed – Stuart found himself surrounded and escaped at the last second by jumping his horse over a wide ditch. At the end of the engagement, there were 215 Federal and 117 Southern casualties. Burdened by a column of captured prisoners and wagons (whose Yankee drivers were in no hurry), Stuart struggled back, looking for Lee. He wasted the bulk of 1 July in sporadic shelling of the town of Carlisle, Pennsylvania, whose militia had refused to surrender. Receiving word of Lee's location at last, he hurried back toward a town called Gettysburg. That day the greatest battle ever seen on American soil had begun without Jeb Stuart.

The battle had spluttered into life when a force of Rebels marched toward Gettysburg to see if they could find shoes – many Confederate soldiers were barefoot. West of town they had run into a detachment of John Buford's cavalry, who dismounted and peppered the Rebels with their Spencer repeating carbines while the Federal infantry moved up. Piece by piece, both armies began pitching units into the battle until a gigantic engagement, planned by neither side, was raging west of Gettysburg. The first day of fighting went well for the South; Union forces were driven back across the town to defensive positions on Cemetery Ridge and the flanking hills. But those Union positions, arrived at by accident after a rout, were to spell disaster for the Confederacy.

On the second day of the battle (2 July), Stuart's men were too exhausted to fight. In the infantry actions of that day, Lee's attacks went off haltingly and piecemeal; by a thread, Union General Meade's army held its line. Next day Lee decided to try and smash the Union center by an infantry charge of 15,000 men. That effort, known to history as Pickett's Charge, was

Above; *The Battle of Chancellorsville.*

doomed from the outset by the impenetrable Union position on Cemetery Ridge. But while that charge, the high-water mark of the Confederacy, was taking its tragic course, there were separate cavalry battles on both flanks, battles that in some ways were just as critical to the outcome.

While Lee's grand charge was moving on the Federal center, Stuart had been ordered to cut Meade's communications on the Union right. If this were accomplished, Meade would have to draw off infantry to protect his rear. Confidently, the brigades of Wade Hampton and Fitz Lee, still schooled largely in victory, moved to the attack. Opposing them were the Federal Cavalry of D M Gregg, J I Gregg, J B McIntosh and a young and impetuous general named George Armstrong Custer.

The Federals watched the Southern horsemen approaching in close columns of squadrons, as if on parade. Then Union artillery belched a storm of double canister into the Rebel line, turning its front rank into a mass of floundering men and horses. The Southern officers shouted 'Keep to your sabers, men!' and ordered the charge,

straight toward a Michigan outfit. At the head of the Blue cavalry rode General Custer, who watched the enemy galloping toward him for a moment before standing in his stirrups and shouting 'Come on, you Wolverines!' The two lines crashed together with the sound, one observer recalled, of a great tree falling. Quickly the fight broke up into a confused melee of individual struggles, charge and countercharge, units fighting sometimes mounted and sometimes dismounted. Wade Hampton went down with a saber cut on his head. As the hours wore on and his men fell in dozens, Jeb Stuart anxiously awaited word that Pickett's charge had broken through the Federal center. The word never came.

Stuart's battle died down inconclusively in the late afternoon; he had not achieved his objective of cutting Meade's communications. Over on the Union right, a foolhardy charge by Judson Kilpatrick's Union Cavalry had been cut to pieces by Southern infantry. Finally, Stuart's men gave up and rode to the rear. The greatest and most terrible battle on American soil was over.

Above: Panicked and wounded horses struggle in their traces at the Battle of Gettysburg.

Opposite: Major General George A Custer (left) with General Alfred Pleasanton. Custer's Civil War record was far more impressive than his subsequent role on the Western frontier.

For the Army of Northern Virginia it was, at last, a day of complete and unmitigated defeat. And partial blame for that defeat must be laid at the door of Jeb Stuart, whose raid had blinded Lee at the most critical moment of the war. Now it was to be the turn of the Union Cavalrymen, and especially of a little Irishman named Philip Sheridan.

Lee's stricken forces pulled back into Virginia. They were to go on fighting for nearly two years more, but never again with such strength and confidence. The South was running out of soldiers and its cavalry out of horses. While Lee was losing at Gettysburg, Grant was seeing victory in his long campaign against Vicksburg, Mississippi. In both the Eastern and Western theaters the war had turned against the Confederacy that July, and it would never really turn back. Jeb Stuart and his cavalrymen still had much hard riding to do, including the Wilderness Campaign that was followed by Spotsylvania, but now it was too late for the Cavalier or anyone else to stop the Federal juggernaut. All Stuart's riding would only bring him closer to a place called Yellow Tavern.

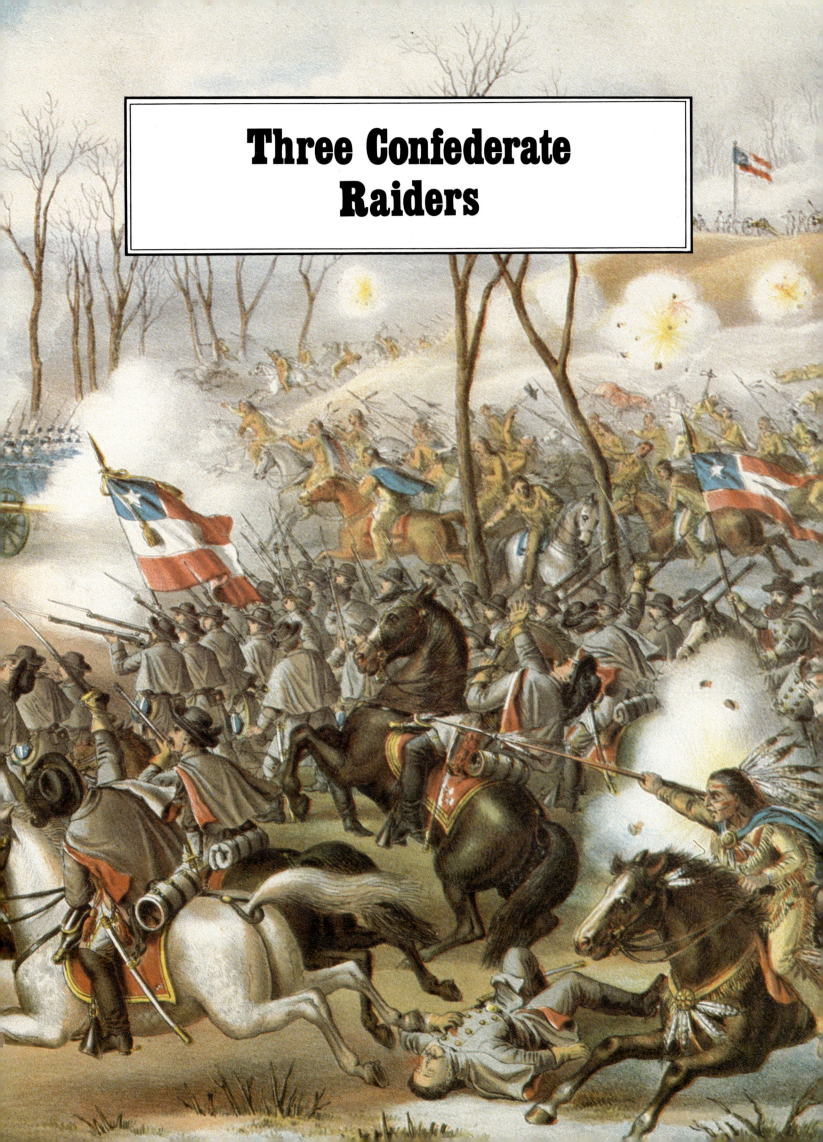

Three Confederate Raiders

Previous pages: *The Battle of Pea Ridge, Arkansas, March 1862.*

Left: *Colonel John S Mosby, who carved out 'Mosby's Confederacy' with his raiders.*

The highly irregular career of Southern irregular John Singleton Mosby may be said to have begun with a stint in jail, where he landed after shooting a fellow University of Virginia student during a fracas. In jail Mosby began reading law with his defense counsel and after his release went into legal practice. When the Civil War broke out, Mosby, then 28, joined a Virginia cavalry outfit and from there hitched up with Jeb Stuart's command, for which he acted as a guide on Stuart's first ride around McClellan and on a number of other operations.

Too restless and independent to be content with riding in Jeb Stuart's shadow, Mosby gained permission in January of 1863 to form a group of raiders to operate in Virginia. It was then that he became the Mosby known to history – the most successful guerrilla fighter of the war. He and his men were officially dubbed Partisan Rangers and given formal status in the Confederate Army – this in an effort, usually successful, to keep them from being hung as spies and looters when captured. But from the beginning the group functioned informally, free of the usual military protocol – only Mosby was ever saluted or addressed by his rank, uniforms were *ad hoc* and aside from a great deal of shooting practice, there was never any drill. The band soon became known to friend and foe alike as 'Mosby's Irregulars,' and their usual territory of operations in Virginia was 'Mosby's Confed-

Above: *Union Cavalry scouting near Fairfax Courthouse, Virginia, after a skirmish that saw 30 of their number captured or killed.*

Opposite: *Mosby's raiders capture and loot a Union wagon train carrying supplies, as seen in an 1863 issue of* Harper's Weekly.

eracy.' Wearing a feathered hat second only in fame to Jeb Stuart's, Mosby himself was dubbed 'the Grey Ghost.' In effect, he and his Irregulars had themselves a nice private war for the duration; in the end they were never captured and never surrendered, but simply disbanded and melted back into the countryside. In this they were the closest thing in the Civil War to the band led by Francis Marion, the Swamp Fox of the Revolution.

Like Marion's men, Mosby's raiders galloped out on hit-and-run missions, each man armed with two or three six-shooters, and spent most of their nonworking time at home or as guests of friendly farmers. Thus, in contrast to most Confederate soldiers, they ate well throughout the war. Their accoutrements were similarly luxurious; in later years an old Irreular recalled, 'We had ups and downs; but after our successful raids we were the best dressed, best equipped, and best mounted Command in the Confederate Army.... Union army sutlers supplied us with a varied assortment of luxuries, and I cannot recall an instance when we rejected what they had on hand or when we threatened to take our trade to some competitor.' Indeed, the primary draw for joining on with Mosby was the food and the loot. Foraging from civilians was forbidden, but anything Yankee was fair game, and after a raid the haul was divided among all (a captured Union payroll once provided $2100 in crisp new greenbacks for each raider).

During their first couple of months, the Ir-

regulars worked in obscurity, often functioning as an advance for Jeb Stuart and stealing Yankee horses for his cavalry. But in March of 1863, Mosby and his men hit the headlines North and South with their raid on Fairfax Court House. There, on the night of 7 March, Mosby and 39 partisans threaded their way between Federal guards, cut the telegraph lines and then transformed themselves into a 'Federal' patrol. Asleep in his bed, Union general Edwin H Stoughton was shaken awake by a slap on his bare behind and found himself confronting a group of strangers. Stoughton demanded to know the meaning of this, and got his reply from Mosby himself: 'It means, sir, that Stuart's cavalry are in possession of this place, and you are a prisoner.' With Stoughton and 31 other captured Federals in tow, plus 58 horses, the raiders slipped quietly back out of Union lines. Their only close call came when a Union colonel challenged them from an open window; seeing enemy soldiers materialize at his door, the colonel hightailed it out the back 'in a nude state' and hid under the privy. No doubt Jeb Stuart roared with his famous laughter when he heard the report.

From then on, Mosby's name would frequent the headlines. Under the twin lures of loot and adventure, hundreds flocked to join his band, somtimes deserting other Confederate outfits to do so. Eventually, Mosby mustered some 1000 men under the designation of the 43rd Virginia Cavalry Battalion, but most of his raids used

fewer than 300, and Irregulars they remained.

When in June 1863 Lee needed information about Hooker and the Army of the Potomac, Mosby got his news by the simple expedient of riding through the enemy's camps. Later in the year Stuart sent Mosby to operate against a rail crossing at Warrenton Junction, behind Union lines in Virginia. The Irregulars burned all the culverts and trestles they could get to, then headed for Catlett's Station with a captured howitzer. Next day they cut the telegraph wires, pulled a rail from the track, aimed the howitzer down the line, and awaited developments. When the Federal train appeared, it ran off the track at top speed where the rail had been removed. The Federal guard of 200 men was sent on their way by a round of grapeshot from the howitzer. Finally, the Federals pitched into the tiny group of Irregulars and chased them away, but the Union suffered 12 casualties to Mosby's one loss.

During Sheridan's Shenandoah Valley Campaign of 1864, Grant, tired of his operations being bedeviled by Mosby's band, ordered the Irregulars hanged without trial if captured. The order was followed only once, by George Custer, who captured six of Mosby's men, hanged a couple and shot the others. Mosby sent word to the Federals that he'd retaliate eye for eye, then hanged six Yankees. Thereafter, Grant's order was ignored.

So it went through the long months of the war, the Grey Ghost and his partisans remaining

supreme in Mosby's Confederacy to the end. During the Wilderness Campaign, Grant diverted a good number of men in efforts to bring Mosby to bay; they never succeeded, though Irregular operations were reduced after Sheridan's campaign in the Shenandoah. As noted earlier, Mosby and his Rangers were never caught and never surrendered, but ended their

Top: *Battle of the Wilderness 5–6 May 1864.*

Above: *Todd's Tavern – Sheridan's cavalry vs Stuart's. Six days later, Stuart would die at the age of 31.*

It Went Against Us, *by Samuel J Reader, one of many American artists who were inspired by the immense national tragedy that was the Civil War.*

Right: *Reader's depiction of a charging Confederate horseman titled* Kill the Yanks – Shoot Them!

private war on their own terms. Later a former Union general was to call Mosby's operations 'the only perfect success in the Southern army.'

In his long postwar career Mosby remained unpredictable, not least in his friendships. In his *Memoirs*, U S Grant wrote of the man he had once ordered hanged: 'Since the close of the war, I have come to know Colonel Mosby personally and somewhat intimately. He is a different man entirely from what I had supposed.... He is able and thoroughly honest and truthful.' In fact, Mosby was an active Republican canvasser in Virginia when Grant ran for president. He was rewarded by President Grant with an ambassadorship to Hong Kong. After working in a series of government posts, including the Department of Justice, the Grey Ghost died in Washington in 1916. From beginning to end, from jail to the Justice Department, Mosby was one of a kind.

When the war broke out, John Hunt Morgan was the successful proprietor of a hemp and woolen mill in Lexington, Kentucky, and a former volunteer in the Mexican War. After some hesitation, Kentucky elected to stay in the Union despite its slaveholding status. But Morgan, without hesitation, cast his own lot with the South and took a company of militia, which he had founded earlier, to join Albert Sidney Johnston's Confederate Army. Throughout his ensuing career as a raider, he would command mainly Kentuckians. As with Mosby, Morgan's men eventually included deserters

Top: *Morgan's raid on Paris, Kentucky, where 'contributions' were demanded from the inhabitants.*

Above: *Morgan and his men on the march. They were feared and respected for their hard-riding raids.*

Right: *Before the Civil War, John Hunt Morgan was a successful Kentucky businessman who led a militia troop called the Lexington rifles.*

from other Confederate Armies who were attracted by the prospect of adventure and loot.

In the Battle of Shiloh (April 1862) in Tennessee, Morgan commanded the Kentucky Squadron of Cavalry as its colonel. Already the soldiers in his division were calling themselves Morgan's Men. It was after that battle that he made his first raid, taking 325 men on a small but successful jaunt into Tennessee, where they captured and burned much Union matériel. Soon Morgan had a mounted regiment and prepared to make a career as a guerrilla fighter. In July of 1862 Morgan mounted his first major operation. With 800 men, he left Knoxville and headed for Kentucky, capturing a post of Yankee cavalry at Tomkinsville and a couple of Union depots. He continued on to Cynthiana, where he got into a sharp engagement with some Unionist Kentucky militia and pulled back. By the time he returned to Tennessee, he and his men had ridden over 1000 miles in 24 days, captured and paroled 1200 prisoners and lost fewer than 100 men. He had also upset a planned Federal invasion of Chattanooga and made himself a permanent headache to Federal strategists in the vicinity.

In most of his campaigns, Morgan's soldiers fought with revolvers on horseback, but more often dismounted to use their rifles. Morgan was old-fashioned enough to prefer muzzle-loading rifles, claiming that with them soldiers were less inclined to waste their shots. In practice this was manifestly not true: statistically speaking, during the war it took about one man's weight in lead to kill one enemy, regardless of the type of weapon – thus the quantity of fire was more significant than the quality. Like Jeb Stuart, Morgan always brought along horse artillery on his operations.

In October, following Confederate General Bragg's abortive invasion of Kentucky, Morgan went out with 1800 men on his second big raid into his home state. Virtually without opposition, his brigade rode all over Kentucky capturing Federal outposts and tearing up the railroads. At the end of the year, he operated against Federal communications and supplies in Tennessee, destroying some $2,000,000 worth of Federal property. With these successes under his belt, Morgan got very ambitious indeed – too ambitious, as it turned out: he decided to invade the North, to raid Ohio and Indiana.

The ostensible strategic purpose of this raid was to relieve pressure on Confederate Armies in the South after the fall of Vicksburg, which was then imminent. Among other worrisome problems, a Union Army under William S Rosecrans was heading toward Chattanooga. Ohio was also the most active area for Northern Democrats sympathetic to the South, who were

A detail of the Battle of Shiloh from a painting by Alonzo Chappell – Union soldiers struggle to recapture a gun.

The Battle of Chattanooga:
General Thomas's charge
near Orchard Knob, 24
November 1863.

PLANTER'S HOTE

Thomas Nast's view of Confederate raiders laying waste a Western town, published in Harper's Weekly *in 1864.*

known as Copperheads; Morgan hoped to stir up these and other Southern sympathizers in the state. The raiders began in good form by chasing a Union Army away from Knoxville, after which Morgan and his 2500 men rode on into Kentucky. Soon they were running into more resistance than they were used to; trying to cross the Green River into Indiana on 4 July, Morgan's forces were repulsed by a fort containing 400 Michigan soldiers under the command of General Henry M Judah. Morgan and his men moved on, raiding and looting as they went (including robbing a bank). They got away from Lebanon, Kentucky, with 400 Federal prisoners and a considerable haul of captured supplies. On 7 July Morgan used two commandeered steamers to take his force across the Ohio River into Indiana.

Riding and raiding most of the day and into the night, Morgan's column headed northwest, brushing local militia out of the way (the Indiana Home Guard suffered 360 casualties, 345 of them missing in action). Confederate saddles spilled over with captured goods. (For some reason no officer could figure out, the favored loot was calico – most of Morgan's raiders carried massive bolts of the cloth on their horses.) Panic spread like wildfire among the civilian populations of Indiana and Ohio, who felt themselves at the mercy of an unpredictable enemy.

In short, things were going well for the raiders early in the campaign. Morgan had with him an expert telegraph wiretapper who kept him abreast of Union efforts to stop him and in return sent phony messages to Federal commanders; one of the messages falsely warned that Nathan Bedford Forrest, a name feared at least as much as Morgan's, was coming to reinforce the raiders. At this, the Union command in the area sank into utter confusion. By 13 July the raiders were in Ohio, still riding day and night. However, the rigors of the campaign were taking their toll on horses and men alike; the column was now reduced to about 2000, and exhausted mounts had to be exchanged for commandeered horses, some of them unshod. Learning that Federal troops under generals Judah and Burnside were waiting for him in Cincinnati, Morgan took his men through the suburbs of the city in pitch darkness. During the night, riders in his trailing columns had to stop at intersections, get down on hands and knees and, since there were hoofprints going in every direction, try to figure out which trail had the freshest horse slaver and manure so they could follow their leading column (as good an example as any of the often-unromantic side of soldiering in those days).

By the time Morgan and his men made it to Williamsburg, Ohio, they had ridden and

Left: *John Morgan's Raiders charge an impromptu barricade in a woodland attack.*

marched 90 miles in 35 hours and were beyond exhaustion. They rested there a few hours before pulling wearily away. It was at that point that Morgan's luck began to run out. He was harassed by state militia and encountered stiff Federal resistance at Pomeroy, in southeast Ohio. On the 18th the raiders stopped in Buffington; Morgan had intended to recross the Ohio River at the town but found some Federals forted up and ready to resist. Next morning the Rebels mounted an attack on the fort only to find the defenders gone. However, the Yankees turned up again soon enough – some 10,000 of Judah's troops, supported by gunboats on the river, attacked Morgan, boxed his force into a valley, and whipped him badly. About 120 of the raiders were killed and 700 captured. With 300 men Morgan retreated north toward Pennsylvania. His rearguard, who were out of ammunition, stood off the pursuing Federals with swords.

With Judah's Federals in hot pursuit, Morgan and his remaining men somehow made it some 200 miles to the northeast before being brought to bay. Near New Lisbon, 10 miles from the Pennsylvania border, Morgan and 365 officers and men surrendered. It had been the best of raids and the worst of raids. The Confederates had accomplished a phenomenal feat of endurance, averaging 21 hours a day in the saddle since entering Ohio. On the other hand, their entire force had been annihilated on a mission of dubious value. As a later commentator wrote, 'This reckless adventure . . . deprived [Morgan] of his well-earned reputation.'

It was nearly the end of Morgan's contributions to the Confederate cause, but not quite. In November 1863 Morgan and a few of his officers tunnelled out of a Federal prison in Columbus, Ohio, and made their way back to Kentucky. They were received with general rejoicing, and in 1864 Morgan was given command of the District of Southwestern Virginia. Dozens of his old raiders began filtering back to join him. After

fighting an inconclusive battle in Wythe County, Virginia, Morgan tried another raid into Kentucky with 1000 men (400 were on foot for lack of horses). For a while Morgan seemed to have regained his old dash; he outrode Union detachments in the hills of Appalachia and began cutting railroads and telegraph lines and burning bridges. But on 9 June Union General Stephen Burbridge jumped Morgan's column and repulsed it with heavy losses. The Confederates retreated to Lexington, where Burbridge trounced them again the next day. Desperately, Morgan straggled on with his remaining raiders, who began looting like common bandits.

On 4 September Federal General A C Gillem surrounded Morgan's last contingent in their bivouac at Greeneville, Tennessee. The Rebels tried to break out and 100 were killed. Among the dead was John Hunt Morgan. He had made a brilliant start in the raiding business, but his ambitions had outrun achievable goals – unlike Mosby, whose realism made him the more successful raider. On the other hand, maybe Morgan was simply unlucky – luck playing a far greater role in military matters than is usually admitted. In any case, by the time of Morgan's death the war was virtually over.

Above: *Confederate cavalry leader John Mosby reviews his horsemen, still 600 strong, on 21 April 1865.*

Below: *Nathan Bedford Forrest, whom Confederate General J E Johnston would describe as the greatest soldier of the Civil War.*

There is no doubt that Nathan Bedford Forrest was one of the great military geniuses of the war; the question is, where did his genius come from? Not only did Forrest have no military training (the majority of the war's officers on both sides were West Pointers), he had hardly any schooling at all, and his spelling was as rough as his speech. Born into a poor white family, Forrest went on to a business life that included slave dealing (and for all their willingness to fight and die for slavery, most Southerners looked down on the slave trade itself). By the time the war broke out, Forrest had raised himself quite high by his bootstraps, having progressed from selling slaves to selling real estate in Memphis. As Forrest later said, 'I went into the army worth a million and a half dollars and came out a beggar.' The most famous quote attributed to him, however, is of doubtful authenticity but has survived as a succinct summary of military strategy: 'Git thar fustest with the mostest.' Throughout his military career, Forrest was to show his genius mainly in his ability to maneuver inferior forces into local superiority over the enemy.

With the coming of the war, Forrest raised a mounted regiment out of his own pocket and became its colonel.

His men were outfitted with pistols and shotguns rather than sabers and usually dismounted to fight. Soon Forrest was in charge of eight companies, some 650 men. They saw little action until the end of 1861, when he and his forces routed some Union Cavalry in Sacramento, Kentucky, where Forrest maneuvered the enemy into defeat, showing for the first time his intuitive tactical skills. In February of 1862, Forrest's division was inside Fort Donelson on the Mississippi during Grant's siege. The fort had been starved out, and the Confederate generals voted to surrender; Forest refused to surrender and got permission to try to fight his way out. Somehow he led a column of 200 men through the Federal lines to safety: these were

the only troops Grant did not capture.

Two months later Forrest was fighting Grant
again as commander of a regiment at the Battle of
Shiloh in Tennessee. Placed in reserve, Forrest
moved up on his own tack during the first day's
fighting to help wipe out a pocket of Union resistance in the Hornet's Nest. That night he tried
to convince his superiors to attack the Federal
reinforcements that were arriving steadily; the
generals refused, and next day Grant used those
reinforcements to send the Rebels into retreat
after their first day's victory. That day Forrest's
regiment fought dismounted in the middle of
the Confederate lines, then covered the rear
during the retreat. His regiment broke up
Sherman's advance with their shotguns, chasing
the bluecoats back to the main line. It was
Sherman's first encounter with the man destined to be his *bête noire*. Finally, Forrest charged
the Yankees singlehandedly and was badly
wounded; in fact, it was declared a fatal wound,
but he was back in action three weeks later.

Forrest was made a brigadier general in the
summer of 1862, with command of 1400 troops.
On 13 July he led them against a large Federal
depot at Murfreesboro, Tennessee; half the
Federals ended up as casualties, the other 1200 as
prisoners. It was the first of many raids, most of
them in Tennessee, for Forrest and his 'critter

company,' actions that would make life considerably less pleasant and more dangerous for
Union soldiers in the South.

In the spring of 1863 a Union Army under
Rosecrans was deadlocked with the forces of
Confederate General Braxton Bragg in middle
Tennessee. The raids of Forrest and Morgan had
made the Federal position tenuous. To deal with
this, Federal Colonel Abel Streight was sent out
with a mule-mounted command to draw off the
Rebel raiders. Streight's column headed into
Alabama in mid-April. Soon Forrest was on
their trail, telling his men to 'Shoot at everything
blue and keep up the scare.' The Rebels did so,
and Streight found Forrest's men apparently as
thick as the trees. The Federal column limped
east across Alabama, fighting incessantly.
Finally, on 3 May, Streight gave in to the inevitable and met with Forrest under truce to
discuss surrender terms. During the conversa-
tion Forrest had his forces, which were about a
third of the Federals', circle around and around a
hill until Streight exclaimed, 'Name of God!
How many guns have you got? There's fifteen
I've counted already.' There were, in fact, two
cannons. When Streight found out he had surrendered 1466 prisoners to a force of 500, the
Union colonel was outraged and demanded that
Forrest give him back his men and fight it out.

General Ulysses S Grant
leads the charge at the
Battle of Shiloh, 6–7 April
1862.

Right: *Jefferson Davis, President of the Confederate States of America, looked like an aristocratic planter, but came from a farming family of modest means. He attended West Point at the same time as Robert E Lee.*

'Ah, Colonel,' Forrest drawled, 'all is fair in love and war, you know.'

Nemesis that he was to his enemies, Forrest had nemeses of his own – namely, the Confederate command structure, which never seemed to recognize his brilliance. Confederate President Jefferson Davis had a remarkable talent for holding down good generals and promoting bad ones. Though Forrest was spared the fate of first-rate generals like Beauregard and J E Johnston, who were ignored for much of the war, his superiors had the habit of rewarding his successes by taking his outfit away from him. Still, Forrest always ended up with another command, and always led it to victory. Given Forrest's fiery temper, there were inevitable problems with subordinates as well, one of whom shot Forrest during an argument in June 1863. Forrest grabbed the officer's pistol hand, held it fast while he opened a penknife with his teeth and stabbed his assailant mortally. In the fall of that year, Forrest watched his superior Braxton Bragg win the Battle of Chickamauga and then let the Yankees get away to Chattanooga without a chase.

In a perfect fury, Forrest screamed at Bragg, 'You commenced your cowardly . . . persecution after Shiloh, because I reported to Richmond facts, while you reported damned lies. You robbed me of my command that I armed and equipped from the enemies. You are a coward and a damned scoundrel. You may as well not issue any more orders to me, for I will not obey them. For some reason Bragg did not have Forrest called up for insubordination – perhaps because Forrest was irreplaceable, perhaps because Bragg suspected he was right. In any case, Forrest went raging off to Richmond, where Jefferson Davis gave him another independent command.

On 12 April 1864, Forrest and his division surrounded Union Fort Pillow, which lay on the Mississippi in Tennessee. Having established his men so they could attack the fort without coming under fire themselves, Forrest asked for surrender, but the Union commander declined. The ensuing Rebel attack was swift and successful, with only 90 casualties. But what happened next was as inglorious as anything in the war. Half the Union defenders of the fort were black. During the action over 200 of these black soldiers died, more than twice the number of whites.

The details remain shrouded in mystery, but it seems most likely that the blacks were deliberately slaughtered, many of them after surrender.

Northern survivors reported the Confederates screaming 'No quarter! Kill the damned niggers; shoot them down!' After the battle Forrest wrote in a letter, 'The river was dyed with the blood of the slaughtered for two hundred yards ... it is hoped that these facts will demonstrate to the Northern people that Negro soldiers cannot cope with Southerners.' Despite official Southern denials, the North erupted into accusations of massacre. History has largely supported those accusations.

Thereafter, Forrest made a specialty of hounding the supply lines of Union General W T Sherman, who was pushing south toward Atlanta in the spring and summer of 1864. With increasing frustration, Sherman sent forces after Forrest, only to have them return empty-handed. Meanwhile, the Federal supply line became longer and more vulnerable by the day. At the beginning of June, Sherman was howling 'That devil Forrest must be hunted down and killed if it costs ten thousand lives and bankrupts the Federal treasury!' Sherman sent out a detachment of 3000 cavalry, 4800 infantry and 18 cannons under General S D Sturgis to do the hunting and killing.

As always, Forrest did not wait for the enemy but took the offensive himself, though he had available only 4713 men and 12 cannons. Learning of Sturgis's approach to Brice's Cross Roads

General Grant was widely criticized for the heavy Union casualties at the Battle of Shiloh, but Lincoln came to his defense. 'I can't spare this man,' said the President. 'He fights.'

Right: *A parley between Generals Sherman and Joseph E Johnston during the last year of the war.*

Below: *Confederates under Nathan B Forrest storm Fort Pillow in April 1864. Colonel Robert McCulloch commanded the left wing of the Confederate force, seen here.*

in Mississippi, Forrest moved his forces up fast and beat Sturgis to the crossroads. On 10 June Forrest was met at the crossroads by General Benjamin Grierson's cavalry, 3200 strong; at that point Forrest had some 900 men in position and his artillery was eight miles back. Nonetheless, Forrest dismounted his troops and sent them forward to attack, making them as visible as possible. The bluff worked: Grierson did not press forward to find how thin the enemy line was. After falling back and finding the Yankees did not advance, Forrest ordered another bluffing attack. Finally, the Confederate artillery and troops began to arrive. When the main Federal column pulled in, exhausted from marching in the fierce early afternoon heat, they found themselves under attack in earnest. With no more than 1700 men actively engaged, Forrest by then had broken through Grierson's center while immobilizing his flanks. By five o'clock in the afternoon, the Confederates were crumpling the flanks of the Federal battle line. At that point the Union forces fell into utter panic and fled; Forrest chased them the rest of the night and next day. With less than half the Federals' numbers, he had beaten them decisively and captured 250 wagons and ambulances, 18 cannons, 5000 rifles, massive quantities of ammunition and the entire baggage train. Sturgis lost 227 killed, 394 wounded and 1623 captured; Southern losses numbered about 492 in all. The Battle of Brice's Cross Roads was 'that devil' Forrest's finest day.

Forrest returned to harassing Sherman's supply line, first clearing East Tennessee of enemy forces. In early November he scared the Federals at Johnsonville into burning vast quantities of supplies and a whole fleet of ships, all of it totaling some $6,700,000 worth of Union property. Despite the success of the Rebel raiders, however, Sherman's advance was inexorable. In November Sherman and his army cut away from their supply lines and set out east across Georgia in their March to the Sea, foraging and burning as they went. Behind them they left Atlanta in ashes. The Union juggernaut had become too much for Forrest or anyone else to stop. In the last days of the war he was made a lieutenant general, but could not halt the Union advance into Alabama; it was his only real loss of the war.

Forrest's later career lacked the glamour of Mosby's. He was associated with the Ku Klux Klan at its formation and became its first Grand Wizard, though he resigned from the organization in 1869. He worked in planting and railroading without regaining his former fortune and died in Memphis in 1877, aged 56. In later years someone asked Confederate General J E Johnston (Sherman's adversary in the Atlanta Campaign) who was the greatest soldier of the war. Without hesitation Johnson named Nathan Bedford Forrest, 'who, had he had the advantages of a thorough military education and training, would have been the great central figure of the Civil War.' Whether or not that is true it was certainly true that, except for Lee's operations, the South was losing on its own territory more often than not throughout the war, and by keeping Forrest in small commands, Jefferson Davis hamstrung the only man who might have been a match for Grant and Sherman. But as with his fellow raiders Morgan and Mosby, Forrest's exploits had an impact far out of proportion to the small number of horsemen he commanded.

The Union Horsemen
Ride to Victory

At the war's beginning the Union command structure was in a state from which it would recover only after three years of rapid command shifts. Guiding Federal operations at the outset was General Winfield Scott, who first saw action in the War of 1812 and was now an aged and debilitated campaigner. Scott had never had much use for cavalry and still did not; echoing an opinion that went back to George Washington, he opined that cavalry was useless in broken or wooded country. Nonetheless, regular-army recruitment went on, mostly in the cities and towns of the North, pulling young Yellowlegs into training camps without worrying too much if they'd ever been acquainted with life on horseback.

In fact, few of the recruits were riders at all, and the camps quickly became scenes of low comedy, as described by one officer who recalled:

The general was sounded, ''Boots and Saddles'' blown, and Major Falls commanded, ''SHOUN! 'AIR T'-A-O-U-N-T!''
Such a rattling, jingling, jerking, scrambling, cursing I never before heard. Green horses – some of them never had been ridden – turned round and round, backed against each other, jumped up or stood up like trained circus horses. Some of the boys had a pile in front, on their saddles, and one in the rear, so high and heavy it took two men to saddle one horse and

two men to help the fellow in his place. The horses sheered out, going sidewise, pushing the well-disposed animals out of position, etc. Some of the boys had never rode anything since they galloped on a hobbyhorse, and clasped their legs close together, thus unconsciously sticking the spurs into their horses' sides . . .

In less than ten minutes the Tenth New York Cavalrymen might have been seen on every hill for two miles rearward. Blankets slipped from under saddles and hung by one corner; saddles slid back until they were on the rumps of the horses; others turned and were on the underside of the animals; horses running and kicking; tin pans, messkettles,

Previous pages: General George B McClellan and the 5th Cavalry crossing Bull Run at Blackburn's Ford.

Above: A Union mule team bogs down and its driver is threatened by a frustrated officer – 'Get that team out of the mud!'

Below: Rush's Lancers – the 6th Pennsylvania Cavalry – as depicted by Winslow Homer from a wartime sketch.

patent sheet-iron camp-stoves, the boys had seen advertised in the illustrated newspapers and sold by the sutlers . . . flying through the air.

These were the recruits with whom the Union Cavalry was about to take on Jeb Stuart.

Aiming for a mounted strength of six regiments, Winfield Scott and his staff reorganized the mounted forces – all of them called cavalry for the first time. The 1st and 2nd Dragoons were now the 1st and 2nd Cavalry, the Mounted Rifles became the 3rd Cavalry, and the old 1st and 2nd Cavalry were renamed the 5th and 6th Cavalry. Hidebound by tradition, Northern generals began the war by ignoring the already-developed breechloading and repeating rifles that, later in the war, would help turn the tide for the Union (and in the process contribute to the obsolescence of mounted soldiers). Thus the Union Cavalry rode to war with sabers strapped under their legs, many of them carrying a muzzle-loading single-shot horse pistol that had a recoil vicious enough to kick the unwary out of the saddle (some men had newer muzzle-loading six-shooters, for which one could carry extra snap-in chambers).

Federal generals' notions of cavalry tactics were equally traditional – just like Frederick the Great's horsemen, the Union Cavalry was primarily intended to function as saber-wielding shock troops. The horseman on the field soon learned, however, that they were more effective in riding to the scene of action and dismounting to shoot – in short, fighting like dragoons.

Another reason Scott downplayed mounted troops was that, since everyone expected a short war, it seemed cavalry was both too expensive and too time-consuming to outfit and train. However, there was a good deal of public pressure for mounted units. Sensitive, as always, to that pressure, President Lincoln authorized any and all volunteers to sign up. This well-intentioned response led to further absurdities. Various men of means assembled their own outfits and received their commissions as officers of volunteers (though some groups elected their officers and, when push came to shove, were apt to find those officers ungrateful and to say so).

The result of all this private initiative was a helter-skelter collection of volunteer outfits sporting such fanciful designations as the Light Horse, Hussars, Dragoons, Mounted Rifles and the like. Many of them were grandly clad, most as green as the hills when it came to fighting. These in turn were ripe prey for crooked horsetraders and outfitters. Contemplating the inevitable chaos, one private wrote, 'The blind led the blind, and often both fell into the same ditch, though not always at the same time.' Not surprisingly, it was to be several years before Federal horsemen were whipped into an effective fighting force.

A Mathew Brady photograph taken at Army of the Potomac headquarters in 1864: Captain Edward A Flint and his mount.

After the Union humiliation at First Bull Run, Lincoln replaced Winfield Scott as commander of Federal Armies with General George B McClellan, a former Dragoon who had studied military science in Europe and brought back his own adaptation of a European military saddle. A lightweight wooden tree covered with rawhide and bristling with hooks and loops for equipment, the McClellan Saddle was made standard issue for Federal Cavalry during the war. McClellan spent only a few months as overall Union commander, but considerably longer as leader of the Union Army of the Potomac, which he built up to be the principal Union Army without being able to lead it to a decisive victory.

McClellan's Army of the Potomac took shape over the end of 1861 and into 1862; it attained a strength of 560 regiments of infantry and 90 of cavalry. Heading the Cavalry Corps was General George Stoneman, 39 years old and, like McClellan, a former Dragoon, veteran of fighting in the West and in Mexico. Described as a figure 'lithe, severe, gristly, sanguine . . . whose eyes flashed even in repose,' Stoneman had been promoted ahead of his old senior officer in the Dragoons, Philip St George Cooke. Cooke probably saw this as the injustice it was, but he was a man who did his duty. One possible reason Cooke was passed over was that he was Virginia-born and all the rest of his family went with the Confederacy – including his daughter, the wife of Jeb Stuart, and his son John, who became a general in Lee's Army. In addition, the rigors of Dragoon life, beginning with the Dodge Expedition, had taken their toll on Cooke's health.

Despite his experience in the Dragoons, General McClellan never used his cavalry as a true fighting unit. Rather, he parceled them out among his other divisions to scout, take messages, guard and often to run errands and police the camp. It was not long before Union infantrymen took up the sardonic and often-repeated gibe, 'Who ever saw a dead cavalryman?'

As mentioned earlier, McClellan and his Army of the Potomac began the Peninsular Campaign in the summer of 1872, moving by ship to the bottom of the peninsula between the York and James Rivers in Virginia and then marching overland toward Richmond. As always, McClellan moved slowly, convinced by his intelligence reports – which came not from his cavalry but from Allan Pinkerton's agents – that he was vastly outnumbered (actual enemy strength was more nearly half his). Exasperated at McClellan's continual demand for reinforcements, Lincoln complained, 'Sending reinforcements to McClellan is like shovelling flies across a barn.' The result of the Peninsular Campaign we have already seen – it accomplished little except to chew up the lives of a great many soldiers. McClellan had not exactly been defeated, but he had been outgeneraled and chased from Virginia. His army was outfought, and Jeb Stuart had ridden circles around him.

After Pope's defeat in the Second Bull Run, McClellan resumed command of the war in the East, still keeping his cavalry subservient and retaining Stoneman as their commander. Although General Pope had given his cavalry their head for a few days before the battle, sending John Buford and others out to raid and scout, the

Above, left: *Union cavalrymen of the 3rd Pennsylvania at Brandy Station, Virginia, scene of the Civil War's greatest cavalry battle.*

Above: *The 7th New York Cavalry encamped near Washington, DC. In the foreground are General I N Palmer and his staff.*

Right: *A Captain of Cavalry, USA, showing saddle equipment and saber.*

White authorities, even sympathetic ones, could only envision one end for the Indians: these peoples of a proud and ancient hunting and fighting tradition were either to be killed or to be herded onto reservations to exist on government handouts until they could be forcibly converted into farmers. The Indians, in short, had to be broken in will and spirit and transformed into small dirt farmers and decent Christians. The fact that this would erase native cultures and religions seemed to most whites to be a positive virtue of the policy. Bewildered, often betrayed, prey to the usually corrupt and indifferent Indian Bureau and to crooked traders and bootleggers, crushed by forces beyond their experience and comprehension, it was for the Indians as if their universe had fallen down on top of them.

Thus a realistic account of this era will not often resemble the exhilarating Hollywood image of the hell-for-leather cavalryman. For the Yellowlegs it was a hard, dangerous and bloody job they were called on to do, much of it dirty work indeed. Yet it had its moments of glory, remarkable feats of heroism on both sides, and now and then even episodes of real understanding, of humanity and justice. In any case, for the horse cavalry it was to be their most difficult and all-but-final, challenge.

At 1:30 AM on 27 November 1868, the Cheyenne village of Chief Black Kettle slept

Right: Posed pictures like this one of two Mojave braves failed to capture the dynamism of the Indian's relationship to the land.

Below: An 1864 recruitment poster for cavalry volunteers: Indian fighting slowed down but never stopped during the Civil War.

along the banks of the Washita River (in what is now Oklahoma). Black Kettle had long been a peace advocate and a pacifying element among his people, but this had not prevented him from being attacked by Chivington in 1864. No matter which Indians went on the warpath, soldiers and settlers were likely to strike back at any Indians handy. This was about to happen to Black Kettle and his people again, and for the last time. A squaw saw soldiers coming and screamed a warning. In another moment a column of US Cavalry roared into the village, pistols blazing, the company band playing away on freezing instruments. Black Kettle, emerging from his tepee, was riddled with bullets. Within a half hour 103 warriors were cut down, 53 women and children taken prisoner. The attacking cavalrymen lost 22 killed and 14 wounded. As was their custom, the Cheyenne warriors mutilated the corpses of their enemies, but before long most of the warriors were dead too, many of them scalped by the cavalrymen. Among the dead were several white captives who had been killed by Indian women when the attack began. All around lay the dead, freezing quickly in the winter cold. It was a successful raid for the 7th United States Cavalry. Its commander, General George Armstrong Custer, was in his element.

Custer's raid was part of a large offensive against the Cheyenne and Arapaho in Kansas and Colorado, where an uprising by those tribes in 1868 had claimed the lives of 117 settlers. Seasoned cavalryman Philip Sheridan was in command of the area. He had taken the offensive after prodding from his superior in Washington, General of the Army William T Sherman, who had said of the Indian offensive: 'The more we can kill this year, the less we'll have to kill next year, for the more I see of these Indians the more I am convinced that they all have to be killed or be maintained as a species of paupers.' This was to prove a succinct summary of the whole progress of the Indian wars. As for Sheridan, the man in charge of operations against the Plains tribes, he was said to have originated the phrase 'The only good Indian is a dead Indian.' After Custer's attack on the Washita, Sheridan considered the Indians in the area properly subdued.

This was the beginning of the final push against the Indians of the West, although it took over 20 more years to subdue the last of the uprisings. Operations in the West had naturally slackened during the Civil War, and Indian power and confidence had grown accordingly in the absence of strong resistance. Still, there was plenty of action and fighting in the West during the war. One non-cavalry endeavor was to become part of American legend despite its short history – the Pony Express, a fast mail service between St Joseph, Missouri, and Sacramento, California, that lasted from April 1860 to the end of 1861. Using chains of horses

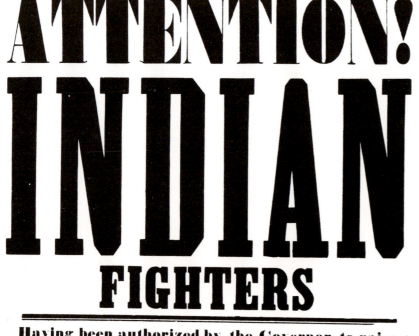

ATTENTION! INDIAN FIGHTERS

Having been authorized by the Governor to raise a Company of 100 day

U. S. VOL CAVALRY!

For immediate service against hostile Indians. I call upon all who wish to engage in such service to call at my office and enroll their names immediately.

Pay and Rations the same as other U. S. Volunteer Cavalry.

Parties furnishing their own horses will receive 40c per day, and rations for the same, while in the service.

The Company will also be entitled to all horses and other plunder taken from the Indians.

Office first door East of Recorder's Office.

HAL SAYR.

Central City, Aug. 13, '64.

and riders stationed in 190 posts, the Express carried the mail an astonishing 250 miles a day. During its short history it was remarkably free from interference by Indians, not to mention from fierce winter weather and wild animals. Among the young riders were men like 'Buffalo Bill' Cody and 'Wild Bill' Hickok. For all the glory and attention the Pony Express has received, however, the service was soon doomed by the coming of the transcontinental telegraph in October 1861.

Another figure of Western legend was fighting in the West during the war years – scout Kit Carson, who led operations against his old friends the Navajos and imposed a bitter relocation on them (though later they were returned to their old area). Also during the Civil War, General H H Sibley tore the Sioux out of their hunting grounds and drove them to the Southwest; it was the beginning of 30 years of war against that proud warrior tribe. In November 1867, cavalrymen in what is now Colorado, led by a fanatical Indian-hating colonel named John M Chivington, pounced on Black Kettle's peaceful village of Cheyenne and Arapaho and massacred 500 of its residents, mostly women and children. Indian fighter Nelson A Miles was later to call the Chivington massacre 'perhaps the foulest and most unjustifiable crime in the annals of America.' It was also very unwise, as it made those tribes among the most resentful and implacable Indian raiders in the country, with decades of suffering and death as a result. Meanwhile, during the war the wagon trains of settlers continued to move into the West. By 1870 there were more whites in Kansas alone than there were Indians in the entire United States.

After the Civil War the US Army faced divided responsibilities with declining numbers of troops. They had to occupy the South, patrol the Mexican border and deal with the Indians. The experienced cavalrymen who wanted to remain in the service gradually moved on to life in the Western outposts, which were scattered around Indian Territory and on the Mexican border. New recruits began coming in, but they were an unpromising lot. Many were immigrants, most had little schooling and, not infrequently, criminal records as well. However drunken and unruly the new Yellowlegs proved on the post, though, they usually did the job in the field.

Top: *Black Kettle's people were attacked again along the Washita River in 1868; this time, the Cheyenne leader lost his life. The 7th Cavalry under George Custer made the raid in reprisal for unrelated uprisings in Kansas and Colorado.*

Above: *US Cavalry troopers at ease in their camp at the base of Gillem's Bluff during the Modoc Wars.*

Right: *Cavalry Lieutenant S C Robertson, Chief of the Crow Scouts.*

Above: *The massacre of five settlers in Meeker County, Minnesota, by Eastern Sioux or Santees (17 August 1862) touched off an Indian war that resulted in hundreds of deaths on both sides.*

Left: *The black 10th Cavalry regiment, commanded by white officers, fought in the Geronimo campaign in 1886; depicted here,* The Rescue of Corporal Scott, *by Remington.*

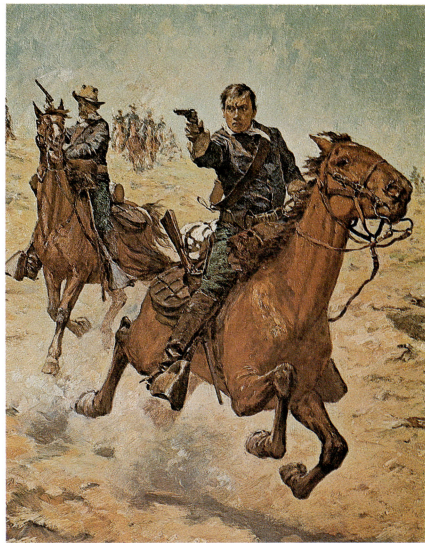

Left: *A US Cavalry column crossing a ford in the last year of the Indian Wars, by Rufus Zogbaum.*

Above: *The short-lived Pony Express mail service between St Joseph, Missouri, and Sacramento, California, galloped into American legend in the early 1860s.*

Top: Dead Sure *by Charles Schreyvogel shows troopers armed with the Colt .45 single-action revolver (1873).*

Frederic Remington
Sierra Bonitas '08

Life on the posts varied in comfort, but was rarely less than difficult. The cavalryman's day was regulated by the post bugler, who sounded Assembly, Recall, Reveille, Mess, Taps, and the many other calls in the repertoire. Summer was filled with mounted and dismounted drill, horse grooming, stable cleaning, inspection, guard duty and the thousand similar chores of military life. A morass of tradition and protocol ruled the procedures of the forts; for example, the old tradition that a new commanding officer could select his own quarters often created a ludicrous shuffling all the way down the chain of command, since everyone lower down got to pick new quarters as well.

Officers' quarters on the posts varied from grim and primitive to spacious and elegant houses like the one in which George and Libby Custer came to rest at Fort Lincoln. The wives faced their own challenges, besides the incessant fear for their husbands' lives. Food supplies often had to come from enormous distances, and women learned to cook without staples like eggs and milk. Children were taught at home before being shipped East to complete their education. In their leisure time, the troops relaxed mainly in the traditional ways – with liquor, gambling and prostitutes. In winter, when there were few duties, boredom became epidemic for the enlisted men, while the officers partied and socialized at an endless series of balls.

On the trail, the horse soldiers scarcely resembled their later Hollywood counterparts. Many wore issue trousers patched with canvas, coats of various issue from the Civil War on, and white or grey felt civilian hats rather than the uniform black campaign hat. George Custer and a few other officers affected fringed buckskins. After 1873 troopers carried that year's Springfield repeating carbine slung on a strap around the body, and a model 1872 Colt six-shooter. Some sported homemade cartridge belts. Sabers were rarely seen.

Four new mounted divisions were created in 1866, when Congress established the 7th through 10th Cavalries. The 9th and 10th consisted of black troopers with white officers. These two outfits were to see as much action as their white counterparts over the coming decades, though they suffered from the racist attitudes that remained endemic in the US Army after the war. Their fighting record was distinguished; indeed, the caliber of black troopers was generally higher than white, since military service represented a rare opportunity for ambitious blacks, while it was often a repository for the dregs of white society. The black cavalrymen came to be called 'Buffalo Troopers,' the name reportedly originating with Indians who first saw the blacks in buffalo robes and thought their hair was also contrived from the

buffalo's hide. The early operations of the Buffalo Troopers were mainly in Kansas and Texas, but later they fought all over the map, earning a number of Medals of Honor in the process. The 9th Cavalry saved the 7th in the aftermath of Wounded Knee, and black troopers fought beside Roosevelt at San Juan Hill.

The cavalry horse Comanche, sole survivor of the battle at the Little Big Horn.

Opposite, top: *General Custer (in fringed buckskins) at Fort Abraham Lincoln, Dakota Territory, with staff members and their families.*

Opposite, bottom: *A scout with the Buffalo Soldiers, as sketched by Remington at Sierra Bonitos in 1888.*

Right: The Last of the Redskins, *an engraving by Gautier, depicts the Indian as noble savage. Many 19th-century Americans were deeply disturbed by the injustices perpetrated against the country's original inhabitants.*

Opposite: *The 8th Cavalry was established in 1866 to augment the forces available for multiple post-Civil War duties: occupation of the South, patrol of the Mexican border and Indian affairs.*

Above: *Custer's attack on the Cheyenne village along the Washita River was the major action of Sheridan's winter war of 1868-9.*

As for the Indians, they led their traditional lives as best they could. Many of them were already on reservations by the end of the war. Among the most aggressive of the Plains tribes were the Sioux and Cheyenne in the north, both peoples being superb horsemen. (The Indians, of course, had not had horses until the Spanish and other Europeans brought them to the New World.) Of the Comanches, to the south, an observer wrote, 'Every warrior has a war horse, which is the fleetest that can be obtained, and he prizes him more highly than anything else in his possession.' Painter George Catlin described the horsemanship of the Comanche warrior, who could ride hanging over the side of the animal with one foot hooked over its back: 'In this wonderful position he will hang whilst his horse is at the fullest speed, carrying with him his bow and shield, and also his long lance ... all or either of which he will wield upon his enemy as he passes; riding and throwing his arrows over the horse's back or under the horse's neck.'

All Indians fought as guerrillas, picking their own place and time to engage the enemy. An associate of General George Crook wrote, 'The Apache was in no sense a coward. He knew his business and played his cards to suit himself. He never lost a shot or lost a warrior when a brisk run across the nearest ridge would save a life or exhaust the heavily-clad soldier who endeavored to catch him.' While the Apaches traditionally stole their horses, the Comanches maintained herds sometimes several times larger than the number of people in the tribe.

The Sioux warrior, General George Crook said, 'is a cavalry soldier from the time he has intelligence enough to ride a horse, [and] they can move at the rate of 50 miles a day.' Throughout the Indian wars, those who esteemed the Indians' fighting abilities most were their Army opponents: one of Crook's officers called the Plains Indians 'the finest light cavalry in the world.'

Philip Sheridan took command of the Department of Missouri in 1868, a year before completion of the Union Pacific Railroad prepared the way for thousands more settlers to move in – and for the hunters who would devastate the buffalo herds that were the life of many Indian tribes. Sheridan oversaw military operations across 150,000 square miles of Kansas, Colorado, New Mexico and Indian Territory. For that purpose he had, absurdly enough, only 1200 cavalrymen and 1400 infantry, stationed in 26 forts. Despite the size of his forces, the pugnacious Sheridan immediately took the offensive. Naturally, his initial tactics were derived from his Civil War experience: thus he would send out large bodies of men in an effort to surround hostile tribes. Occasionally, as with Custer's devastation of Black Kettle's village, these tactics worked. But in the field it was finally realized that what worked better were tactics based on Indian style – small, quick and mobile actions stressing hit-and-run raids. Most of the time the cavalrymen rode to the action and then fought dismounted, every fourth man holding the horses.

131

The kind of depredations the Yellowlegs were expected to stop can be seen in three days of Sheridan's record for 1868:

September 1st, near Lake Station ... a woman and child killed and scalped and thirty head of stock run off by Indians; at Reed's Springs, three persons were killed and three wounded; at Spanish Fort, Texas, four persons were murdered, eight scalped, fifteen horses and mules run off and three women outraged; one of these women was outraged by thirteen Indians who afterwards killed and scalped her and then killed her four little children.

September 2nd, on Little Coon Creek, Kansas, a wagon ... attacked by about forty Indians. Three of the [cavalry escort] were badly wounded; three Indians were killed and one wounded.

September 4th, Major Tilford, 7th Cavalry, Commanding Fort Reynolds, Colorado, reported four persons killed, the day before, near Colorado City. A large body of Indians also attacked the station at Hugo Springs, but were repulsed by the guards.

Above: *General George Crook learned his tactics from his Indian adversaries – who were often his friends. He was universally respected on the frontier in a career that spanned a quarter of a century, after his service in the Civil War.*

Opposite, bottom: *Navajo chief Manuelito was the last holdout against Kit Carson's removal of the Navajos to Bosque Redondo, on the Pecos River in Texas. This photo was taken in Washington, DC, during negotiations with the US Government.*

Against such threats hanging over settlers in the West, it was the cavalry above all who had to take action. But they operated in a maze of conflicting pressures: the demands of fearful settlers to wipe out the Indians once and for all; the demands of pro-Indian forces (of which there was a small but steady element) for justice and restraint; the political pressures to keep a good face on things, even when Indian land was blatantly being stolen. Surprisingly, it was sometimes the soldiers who were closest to the Indians and whose word was most trusted by their enemies – between soldier and Indian there was a certain bond of mutual respect and sometimes outright admiration. This peculiar situation is nowhere better seen than in the career of the greatest Indian fighter of all, General George Crook.

A West Point classmate and friend of Philip Sheridan's, Crook first went to Indian country in 1866 as an Indian commissioner in Oregon. In that booming territory, he developed the tactics that would lead him both to unprecedented victories over Indians and, paradoxically, to becoming one of their greatest friends and champions. To begin with, Crook had a genuine love for many of the Indian ways of life, which he studied tirelessly. He befriended the Indians, riding and eating with them. In contrast to most soldiers, he looked at his enemies as individuals, and quickly showed tribesmen that he was fair and honest; they knew George Crook would punish only the guilty and would always be willing to talk. He also studied everything about the countryside, making sure he knew the terrain, the biology, the botany. Thus on his campaigns Crook generally knew where to find game for his soldiers and grass for his horses.

But Crook's most original and controversial

The Cavalry Moves into the Twentieth Century

Previous pages:
American forces (Rough Riders in foreground) hoist their flag after the surrender of Santiago, Cuba, in the Spanish–American War.

Below: *Cavalry officer and enlisted men in turn-of-the-century full-dress uniform.*

Bottom: *This 2nd-Cavalry mount was a 23-year veteran when he was retired in 1897.*

With the final defeat of the Sioux at Wounded Knee and the disappearance of the American frontier, America began directing some of its energies beyond its borders in a movement destined to see the United States emerge as a world power. Few periods in American history have witnessed such rapid technological growth and such fundamental change in national policy.

For the US Cavalry, the years following the Indian Wars saw some basic improvements. In addition to new drill regulations, already underway, the Regular Cavalry and one regiment of Volunteers were equipped with the .30-caliber Krag-Jörgensen magazine carbine, sporting a cartridge containing smokeless powder and a muzzle velocity of about 2000 feet per second. And for the first time in nearly 50 years, peace reigned in the American West. After Wounded Knee troopers continued to patrol the plains and mountains and track down renegades, but only two minor Indian rebellions required more serious cavalry attention, and neither approached a major encounter. In 1898 the Chippewas of Minnesota had a small skirmish with troopers, and in 1907, when the Utes in Colorado and Utah refused to send their children to school, the entire 6th Cavalry regiment was sent to play truant officer and enforce the law. Veterans remarked that the sympathies of the troopers appeared to be with the children whom they dragged in kicking and screaming to education and civilization. But before the mounted service settled too comfortably into the routine of garrison life, civil troubles erupted in the cities and industrial centers of the rapidly expanding nation. Between 1886 and 1895, the US Army intervened in 328 labor disputes and related disturbances in 49 states and territories, and the horse soldier was often called upon to preserve order. But the next real fighting the cavalry saw came with the Spanish-American War in 1898.

By then the cavalry, with its unequaled tradition and proud officers and men, had become the top choice of many high-ranking cadets at West Point, and was clearly the glamor organization of the US Army. Even so, technological progress was making the horse obsolete. While the internal-combustion engine was preparing to burst upon the scene to alter the face – and the course – of civilization, the range, accuracy and rapidity of modern arms placed cavalry in a position inferior to that of artillery and infantry. With machine guns able to stop a cavalry charge at 2000 yards and artillery at 3500, frontal assault by horse troops was a thing of the past; indeed, the Napoleonic Wars were the last in which horsed cavalry were used as the principal assault troops on a battlefield. In Europe, the use of heavy or assault cavalry, a product of feudalism and chivalry, died hard in Europe in the face of rifles and machine guns. American cavalrymen, however, acknowledging the effects of modern weapons, asserted that

Below: *First Cavalrymen at Fort Grant, Arizona, pass their off-duty hours playing draw poker.*

the mounted arm was still essential, and proved it by employing cavalry in flanking, screening and reconnaissance, and in the guerrilla-style tactics used against the Indians of the West. With artillery taking over the function of heavy cavalry in attack, and modern armored mechanized mounts – that is, tanks – still decades away, infantry might be the most important arm on the field of battle. But it was cavalry that guarded the ammunition, screened, foraged and provided the information necessary to conduct battles. Especially in the 1890s, reconnaissance gained importance. American cavalry, trained to fight mounted and dismounted – combining dismounted fire with the mounted charge – preserved its mobility while adding the firepower of modern infantry.

When insurrection broke out on the island of Cuba in 1895, the American people, who could be expected to favor the aspirations of colonials for independence, sympathized with the insurgents. Their support grew the following year, when newly appointed Spanish governor General Valeriano Weyler attempted to stifle the rebellion by herding noncombatant men, women and children into concentration camps and garrisoned towns where they died by thousands for lack of proper provisioning. Despite rising American public opinion, neither President Grover Cleveland nor his successor William McKinley favored intervention.

America really had no foreign policy, but publication of a letter written by the Spanish minister to the United States, which characterized President McKinley as 'a weakling,' and the 1898 sinking of the US battleship *Maine*, in which 260 Americans lost their lives, gave interventionists the upper hand. Newspapers cried 'Remember the *Maine*!' and the nation sang 'There'll Be a Hot Time in the Old Town Tonight.' An ultimatum was sent to Spain on 27 March 1898; the Spanish Government appeared willing to honor it, but the American people could not wait. Congress passed a joint resolution on 19 April 1898 proclaiming Cuba free and authorizing the president to use force to expel the Spaniards.

The US Cavalry of 1898 was not prepared for war. There were 27,000 enlisted men in the whole US Army, of whom something less than 6000 were cavalrymen. Part of the 3rd Cavalry was at Fort Ethan Allen, Vermont, and part of the 6th at Fort Meyer, Virginia, but most troopers were thinly spread across garrisons in Montana,

Above: Theodore Roosevelt and his Rough Riders on San Juan Hill, Cuba: Colonel Roosevelt was, in fact, the only man mounted for the famous charge against this objective.

Opposite: The inflammatory journalism of William Randolph Hearst and Joseph Pulitzer was a causative factor in the Spanish–American War.

Below: The true cause of the explosion that destroyed the battleship Maine *in Havana Harbor was never determined. Some experts held that the explosion was internal and not attributable to a Spanish mine, as the Americans had charged.*

Wyoming, Colorado, Kansas and other points widely scattered throughout the West. To add to their numbers, a Congressional Act of 26 April 1898 authorized the Regular Cavalry to reactivate two troops in each regiment (from troops deactivated in 1890 or last filled with Indians), and to add a lieutenant, a sergeant, four corporals and 34 privates to each troop. This brought troop strength to 104 and regiment strength to 1262 officers and men. To further increase cavalry power, State Organized Militia units and special Volunteer units were also authorized to muster. This resulted in the formation of three volunteer regiments, only one of which, the 1st United States Volunteer Cavalry, saw action in the war with Spain.

The 1st United States Volunteer Cavalry, also known as the Rough Riders or 'Teddy's Terrors' was created by then Assistant Secretary of the Navy Theodore Roosevelt. It was the last of the 'personal regiments' – elite units raised and officered by a prominent civilian for a particular war, and one of six cavalry regiments active in the West Indies. All cavalry in Cuba fought dismounted: the only man mounted in the historic charge of San Juan Hill was Colonel Roosevelt, and he had to dismount at a wire fence and lead his men to the summit on foot. The charismatic Roosevelt and his colorful troopers captured the imagination of a nation (as well as the interest and attention of the leading war correspondents) that looked upon this war as a glorious national picnic that nearly everyone wanted to attend. Almost forgotten is the role played by then Captain John Joseph Pershing, who guided the 2nd Squadron of the 10th Cavalry up San Juan Hill and earned a Silver Star and a brevet as Major of Volunteers on his way to one of the most distinguished military careers in American history.

So popular was Roosevelt that when news went out that he was forming a regiment, the ranks were filled in less than three weeks (994 enlisted men and 47 officers). Roosevelt chose to serve as lieutenant colonel, second-in-command to his friend Colonel Leonard Wood, Apache fighter and competent Regular medical officer. Principally composed of cowboys and polo players, the Rough Riders also included actors, New York policemen, doctors, frontier sheriffs, prospectors, society leaders, professional gamblers and college athletes. All could ride and shoot. They assembled at a training camp at San Antonio, Texas, in May 1898, and within 13 days the officers organized, equipped and trained a full regiment of horse soldiers – an operation Regular Cavalry outfits were expected to perform in 13 weeks. The Rough Riders shot out lights in local saloons, and at the end of May a high-ranking Regular officer, in whose honor a dress review had been scrupulously prepared, remarked that he had never seen anything worse in his life. In the rush to get to the scene of action, there was no time to procure uniforms, and the regiment at first wore the canvas stable dress of the Regular Cavalry. By the time they reached Cuba, most dressed in the new regulation uniform, which at the time consisted of khaki breeches and blouses with blue flannel shirts (the only remnant of the old all-blue outfit). The

A troop transport ship loading troops for the war zone in Cuba, 1898.

Rough Riders wore red bandanas around their necks. Each trooper was armed with a magazine carbine and a six-shooter revolver. On 29 May the Rough Riders and 1100 horses and mules boarded trains for Tampa, Florida.

The confusion and mismanagement at Tampa was unbelievable. Legend says the regiment had to hold up trains at pistol point to obtain transportation to the docks; history records that they embarked for Cuba by seizing, boarding and holding an unguarded transport which had been assigned to two other regiments. Only eight troops of the Rough Riders ever got on board, and all the horses except those of the high-ranking officers were left behind.

The confusion at Tampa mirrored the confusion at higher levels. The Army had no true general staff, and the United States was preparing to go to war without any co-ordinated plan, without any knowledge of the strength and disposition of either the Spaniards or the Cuban insurgents, without joint Army-Navy planning for an attack on a hostile shore and without any accurate maps of Cuba. If the Spaniards had not been even more inept, the consequences for the United States would have been disastrous beyond imagination.

After sitting for several days in the stifling heat of Tampa Harbor, the American convoy got underway, landing on 22 June at Daiquiri, 18 miles east of Santiago Bay. The plan was to drive into the interior to take Santiago from the rear. The landing, which should have taken hours, took days, and would have been a catastrophe if the Spaniards had organized a determined resistance. Horses were transported ashore by throwing them overboard and letting them swim; several, including one of Colonel Roosevelt's, headed out to sea and drowned. Units got ashore as best they could; at least two men drowned.

After landing safely, the Rough Riders became part of the dismounted cavalry division under former Confederate cavalryman Major General Joseph Wheeler, who had for many years been forbidden to serve in the US Army (in the heat of battle he was heard to refer to the Spaniards as 'damn Yankees'). Wheeler's division consisted of about 3000 troopers composed from the Regular 1st, 3rd, 6th, 9th and 10th Cavalry and the Rough Riders. The 9th and 10th Cavalry were black regiments. Sabers were left behind with the horses, and all fought as infantry, with carbine and revolver. After regrouping, the division pushed ahead on foot into the dense jungle, running into the rear guard of a retiring Spanish force at Las Guasimas on 24 June. There 964 Americans engaged the enemy, winning a victory, with 16 troopers killed and 52 wounded, 8 of the dead and 34 of the wounded being Rough Riders. But the Spaniards had no intention of making a serious stand beyond the outer defenses of Santiago, the most important of which were a long series of ridges known collectively as San Juan. One week later, on 1 July

Top left: *The capture of El Caney, El Paso and the fortifications at Santiago.*

Top right: *Assistant Secretary of the Navy, later President, Theodore Roosevelt was an avid outdoorsman despite asthmatic attacks so severe that he almost died in early childhood.*

Above; *Over half the 35,000 American troops who returned from Cuba had to be treated for malaria, typhoid fever and other tropical diseases at this quarantine camp at Montauk Point, Long Island.*

1898, while the American infantry concentrated on taking the village of El Caney and San Juan Heights, the dismounted cavalry, by way of diversion, stormed the strongly fortified Kettle Hill – the famous San Juan Hill. The Rough Riders dashed ahead of the Regulars of the 1st and 9th Cavalry and caught the first fire from the veteran Spanish infantry's modern Mauser rifles. The Regulars joined the Rough Riders for the final spurt, and the hill was taken. Despite comic-opera overtones, it was a tough fight with heavy losses. Eighty-nine of 490 Rough Riders were killed or wounded, and 375 troopers of 2300 cavalrymen engaged were killed or wounded. Santiago soon surrendered, and all fighting ended in September.

One squadron composed of troops from the 2nd Cavalry mounted on local horses escorted batteries and trains to the front lines at El Caney, and some troopers acted as couriers and litter bearers. In Puerto Rico, Troops A and C of the New York Volunteer Cavalry, also mounted, assisted in a conquest in which there was little bloodshed, no serious hardship and much fun. The Puerto Rican population as a whole received the American troops with enthusiasm.

The Army in Cuba met its worst problems after Santiago surrendered. Malaria, typhoid, yellow fever and unwholesome rations combined to cause such a problem that all American troops, including the Rough Riders, were brought back to an isolated camp on Montauk Point, Long Island, to recuperate. Of the 35,000 who passed through the camp, 20,000 were sick, but most recovered. The Rough Riders were lionized in New York City before being mustered out on 15 September 1898. They presented Roosevelt, who had been promoted to a full colonel shortly before the battle of San Juan Hill, with 'the Bronco Buster,' a statuette specially commissioned from Frederic Remington. So ended the last US Cavalry action of the 19th century.

While the fighting was going on in Cuba, America landed an expeditionary force of about 10,000 men in the Philippines, where native insurgents under their leader Emilio Aguinaldo were attempting to throw off the yoke of Spanish rule. Most Americans had no idea where the Philippines were, and were equally unprepared for the idea of a 6000-mile expedition into the Orient and the establishment of a colonial possession there. Commanded by Major General Wesley Merritt, a cavalryman who had served with distinction under Sheridan during the Civil War, the last military action of the war with Spain was undertaken by infantry who captured the city of Manila in mid-August. Merritt became the first American military governor of the Philippines.

155

Above: *The burning of Manila culminated America's first foray into the Philippines, where cavalryman Major General Wesley Merritt, a Civil War veteran, became the American military governor.*

No cavalry units went to the Philippines in 1898, but, largely at the urging of Major General Wheeler, who went to the Philippines after Cuba, cavalry began to arrive in 1899. By that fall most of the 4th Cavalry had reached the Philippines, and by June 1901, eight Regular cavalry regiments were employed there. After Manila, it had become apparent to the Filipino insurgents that the Americans were there to stay, and early in 1899 they turned against their former allies as they had against Spain. General Wheeler felt cavalry would be more useful in the guerrilla warfare which broke out throughout the islands. In addition to the Regulars, the 11th US Volunteer Cavalry, composed mostly of Americans already in the Philippines, was organized in Manila in the late summer of 1899, and a squadron of volunteer cavalry (eventually known as the Philippine Scouts) was raised among the Filipinos. Aguinaldo's insurrection was primarily a second lieutenant's war, characterized by constant fighting among small units in the jungle and back country. The fighting was bitter and brutal. Between May 1900 and June 1901, the Army fought over 1000 separate engagements in which little quarter

was given or asked; casualties were high. Aguinaldo was captured in March 1901.

Aguinaldo's movement had occurred among the Christian Filipinos of the northern islands, led by the Christian tribe called the Tagalogs. No sooner had the Christian insurgents been subdued than the Muslim Moros of the southern islands rebelled. The Moros were fanatic warriors, hostile to all Christians and heirs of the belief that death in battle against the unbelievers ensured entry into paradise. They were veteran campaigners who had never surrendered some parts of the islands to Spain, and had fought for years against both the Spaniards and the Filipinos. They delayed attacking the Americans because they did not recognize them as Christians.

Under his various titles of Adjutant General, Chief Engineer, Chief Ordnance Officer, Chief Signalman, Captain and Brevet Major, John J Pershing led one of two successful cavalry expeditions into the heart of Moro land. Pershing had learned from fighting Apaches and leading Sioux scouts how important it was to understand the enemy. His knowledge of the Moros – he had taken the time to learn Moro – landed him an important command, and he employed mounted and dismounted cavalry supported by field artillery – howitzers or 'jackass artillery' carried on muleback – to subdue sultanate after sultanate, even in regions that had never heard of Americans or Spaniards. On one occasion he coerced the sultans into signing a peace treaty by threatening to spatter them with pig blood – a defilement that would prevent their entry into paradise. His command of the cavalry gained him the respect of his enemies, who appointed him honorary father of Moro aristocracy and *datu*, or prince, of the Muslim faith. Thirsty for news because the Army was doing its best to censor the American betrayal of Aguinaldo and his government, the media of the day built Pershing into an international hero. President Teddy Roosevelt, who

Opposite top: *General John J Pershing (1860–1948), as painted by Sir William Orpen.*

Above: *The cavalry's second excursion into the Orient came in 1901, when the 6th was dispatched to China as part of an international force to subdue the Boxer Rebellion. These prisoners near Tientsin were brought in by 6th Cavalry troopers.*

could appreciate a competent cavalryman, promoted him to brigadier general over the heads of 862 superior officers. In 1906 he was given command of Fort McKinley, becoming military governor of Mindanao in 1910, from which post he successfully controlled the restless Moros with cavalry, dismounted cavalry and infantry until a permanent peace was achieved in 1913. The Moros, awed by his merciless slaughter of their warriors at Mount Bagsak, where he had used mounted Philippine Scouts to screen combatants from the women and children so that his men could attack without quarter, had by then promoted him from Datu to Sultan Pershing.

Meanwhile, the US Cavalry was instrumental in putting down the Boxer Rebellion in China. At the turn of the century, many Chinese had accepted the teachings of the 'Boxers' (literally, 'the Righteous and Harmonious Fists'), fanatical members of a secret society dedicated to the extermination of 'foreign devils' and the eradication of their influence. The Boxers and their supporters killed hundreds of Westerners and Christian Chinese. After the German minister was murdered on 20 June 1900, and most foreigners took refuge in the British legation

compound in Peking, they were besieged by a force that included some Chinese regular troops. A relief expedition was formed, with American, British, French, Japanese and Russian troops. Major General Adna Ramanza Chaffee, Indian fighter and Civil War cavalryman, commanded the American contingent, which included two squadrons of the 6th Cavalry (most of a regiment) – the same regiment in which he had enlisted as a private in 1861. The 3rd Squadron formed part of the force that stormed the walls of 'the Forbidden City' at Peking, becoming the first white troops to enter the city. This was the first war since the American Revolution in which the Army had co-operated with allies. The Spanish–American War painfully revealed US military inadequacies, but the American role in quelling the trouble in China – made possible by American proximity in the Philippines and involving relatively few troops – was great enough to establish the United States as a strong voice in future Far Eastern problems.

With the end of occupation duties in the Philippines nowhere in sight, Congress authorized an increase in the Regular Army in February 1901. Five new regiments were added

157

to the cavalry, the 11th through the 15th, and enlisted troop strength was authorized to vary from 100 to 164, as directed by the President, the commander-in-chief. Units within the United States were kept to the minimum, while those in the islands were increased as necessary. The cavalry again enjoyed almost a decade of peaceful garrison routine, while regiments took turns serving in the Philippines, Hawaii, Panama and at various stations within the United States, primarily in the West. In between various experiments in cavalry reorganization and employment, a great deal of polo was played, improving horsemanship and the breeding of mounts. In 1904 the Krag-Jörgensen rifle of the Spanish-American War was replaced by the improved bolt-action, magazine-type Springfield 1903, which remained the infantry standard until the beginning of World War II. The Colt automatic .45-caliber pistol was approved in 1911. By the time of the Punitive Expedition into Mexico, all troopers in the United States were armed with it. In 1906 a machine-gun platoon commanded by a commissioned officer was added to each regiment, and during this period the all-khaki or olive-drab uniform became regulation and the blue

The Philippine Islands would prove to be a costly acquisition as the twentieth century unfolded. In 1898, when US soldiers first landed on the islands, few Americans had ever heard of them.

shirt of the Spanish-American War, the last remnant of the all-blue uniform, finally disappeared.

As of 30 June 1915, more than seven full regiments, about one-half of the cavalry, were serving on the Mexican border, as they had been since shortly after the 1910 abdication of Mexican President Porfirio Díaz. Unsettled conditions in Mexico caused by factions vying for power threatened to flow across the border. Two regiments were serving in the Philippines, and one in Hawaii. The cavalry continued to comprise about one-fifth of the total US Army. By 1916 each cavalry regiment was officially organized to consist of a headquarters, a headquarters troop, a supply troop, a machine-gun troop and 12 lettered troops organized into three squadrons of four troops each. Until then, the trooper's life continued to be unmarred by excessive activity, with a few exceptions. During the San Francisco earthquake and fire of 1906, two cavalry regiments under the famous cavalryman and Arctic explorer General Adolphus Washington Greely, commander of all the armed forces on the scene, rushed in to preserve order and aid survivors. In the same year, a three-year intervention in Cuba began, during which two

cavalry regiments formed part of the occupying force. In 1916 the 11th and 12th Cavalry were sent in to restore order in the Colorado mine fields, where there was serious labor trouble involving the famous labor leader Mother Jones. During their stay of nine months, the troopers encountered no difficulties. The next real fighting the cavalry saw began somewhat farther south, in the little border town of Columbus, New Mexico.

At about four o'clock in the morning of 9 March 1916, Mexican bandit-patriot Pancho Villa hit Columbus, New Mexico, which was garrisoned at the time by the 13th Cavalry, with a force of up to 1500 men. Leader of a violently anti-American faction popular in northern Mexico, Robin Hood to many, General Francisco (Pancho) Villa, whose real name was Doroteo Arango, neither smoked nor drank; his critics claimed he was too busy murdering, raping and looting. Villa's raid on Columbus had little military significance, although it greatly enhanced his prestige. It was probably motivated by his anger at the United States for its recognition of his arch-rival Don Venustiano Carranza as *de facto* head of the Mexican government.

Among those attacking Columbus at dawn were undoubtedly Villa's elite 300-man bodyguard, known as *Dorados* because of the gold insignia they wore on their olive uniforms and Stetsons. Mostly Yaqui Indians, each an excellent marksman and superbly mounted, the *Dorados* carried Winchester rifles and two sidearms. Unencumbered by families or camp followers, they were the most mobile of Villa's men, responsible for many of his boldest coups.

Villa's men killed sentries, but they did not enter Columbus without detection. While troopers of the 13th tumbled out of bed – only four troops of the regiment were in town, as the regimental polo team had just returned from a match at Fort Bliss – the *Villistas* rode up and down Broadway, Columbus's main street, smashing, looting and burning. While the dismounted troopers were being rapidly assembled by their officers, the raiders committed what proved to be a tactical error by setting fire to the Commercial Hotel, illuminating themselves for Lieutenant Lucas, commander of the machine-gun platoon, who was having his men set up one of the guns. It jammed. Lucas deployed his remaining guns and troopers as dismounted rifles, posting them so that the *Villistas* were between them and the burning hotel, and opened fire at the perfectly silhouetted Mexicans. Their withering fire took a heavy toll. At the western end of town, where the attack began, the raiders had dragged officers and civilians from their homes or chased them into the mesquite. Several kitchen crews, surrounded in their mess shacks, defended themselves with the shotguns kept on hand to kill quail and rabbits. In one shack the crew used a pot of boiling water, axes and a baseball bat

and actually killed a few of the raiders. It had been a costly raid for Villa. Sixty-seven dead Mexicans were found and burned the next day. American losses totaled seven troopers killed, five wounded; eight civilians killed and two wounded.

As the *Villistas* withdrew, the troopers finally had time to get to their horses. Major Frank Tompkins gathered a mounted detachment of 32 men and pursued the *Villistas* to about 15 miles below the border, sniping stragglers and rearguardsmen with their sidearms, stopping only when their horses played out. Tompkins's

Top: *US troops with casualties of a fight at Mount Dajo, Jolo, Philippines, during the insurrection of 1908–09.*

Above: *Cavalry played a decreasing role in frontal-assault actions from the Napoleonic Wars to the late nineteenth century, while infantrymen increasingly dominated combat as a result of new weapons and technology.*

*Mexican insurrectionist
Pancho Villa on the march
with his soldiers during the
Mexican Civil War.*

even for the peace-seeking Wilson Administration. The day after the raid, President Wilson ordered a Punitive Expedition into Mexico to bring Villa back dead or alive. Wilson, although he had never had a real grasp of Mexican politics, backed Carranza. But like the rest of official America, his administration was much more concerned with the growing war in Europe, particularly deteriorating US relations with Germany, than with the volatile situation south of the border. While at first Carranza appeared to accept America's assistance in chastising his arch-rival (at the time Villa had Carranza more or less besieged in Mexico City), it soon became clear that expecting *Carranzistas* to support an American expeditionary force in Mexico was like expecting Democrats in America to support Mexican invaders gunning for Republicans. Failing to understand that Carranza was only slightly less violently anti-American than Villa, Wilson insisted that the Punitive Expedition proceed with 'scrupulous regard for the sovereignty of Mexico,' and placed so many restrictions on it that the expedition was effectively hampered from the outset. Troopers were forbidden to carry their rifles; their Colt .45 Automatics were their only weapons. Brigadier General John J 'Black Jack' Pershing, chosen to lead the expedition, was forbidden to use the railroads, to enter Mexican towns, or to use the telegraph lines without permission of the Carranza Government, which was almost never granted. Eventually, there was almost as much fighting between the expedition and the *Carranzistas* as between the expedition and the *Villistas*.

Pershing's force of about 5000 troops crossed the border on 15 March 1916, less than one week after Villa rode out of Columbus. Despite the famous photograph of Pershing on horseback leading his mounted headquarters party out of the Santa Maria River, Pershing's mount of choice for the expedition was a black Dodge touring car. Three other Dodges filled with war correspondents and the general's escort followed behind. But the Punitive Expedition was primarily a cavalry expedition with supporting infantry, artillery and various service detachments, including at various times all or parts of the 5th, 6th, 7th, 10th, 11th, 12th and 13th Cavalry. Eight airplanes of the 13 that constituted the entire US Air Force of the day (the 1st Aero Squadron of the Signal Corps, all Curtis JN-2s or 'Jennies') with their 10 officers and 82 men, also joined the expedition. This was their first appearance in a campaign by the US Army; they were primarily used to carry messages. Unfortunately, the planes soon cracked up in the rough Mexican countryside, where replacements and repairs were impossible. Far more notable in their failure on the expedition were the trucks, which also came to grief in the Mexican terrain. Their introduction into the logistics system was a major innovation, and although their mechanical failures occasioned

report estimated that at least another 75-100 raiders were killed by his harassing tactics, bringing total Mexican losses in the raid to nearly 200.

America was outraged. The town of Humboldt, Iowa, put up a $10,000 reward for Villa, dead or alive. Colonel Herbert Slocum, commander of the 13th Cavalry, put up a $50,000 reward from his own money, and George M Cohan wrote a song. The attack was too much

Top: *Colonel George S Patton, Jr, commanded the 5th Cavalry during the second half of 1938 and was a lifelong advocate of the cavalry role in modern warfare.*

Above: *The Colt .45-caliber automatic pistol became standard issue in 1911. General Patton habitually wore a pair of these weapons, earning the nickname 'Pistol Packing Patton.'*

many inconveniences, valuable lessons were learned. Old-fashioned horse- and mule-drawn wagons remained the chief means of supply.

One of General Pershing's aides on the expedition was First Lieutenant George S Patton, Jr, on special service with the command. Known later by his men in Sicily and North Africa as 'Pistol-Packing Patton' because of the pearl-handled revolvers he always wore (he was also known as 'Old Blood and Guts'), one incident in particular demonstrated his ability to use them. While on a foraging mission with seven men in three automobiles, Patton approached a large farm house known to belong to one of Villa's colonels. Patton, believing the colonel might be at home, posted his men at all the exits, covering the front gate to the courtyard himself. Suddenly three horsemen armed with rifles and pistols galloped out of the front gate straight at him. Constrained by the restrictions of the expedition to hold fire until hostile identification was certain, Patton waited until the men fired at him, then killed all three with his pistols. One of the dead horsemen proved to be Villa's colonel.

Pershing split his command into two columns, leading the west column south from Columbus himself. With him went the black 10th Cavalry, the unit he had captained in Cuba; the 7th, an infantry regiment; and a battery of the 6th Field Artillery with three-inch field-pieces. Also with Pershing were the 13th Cavalry with two infantry regiments and another battery of the 6th Field Artillery. The rest of the army moved down on the border, leaving the coast artillery to protect the sea-board. President Wilson federalized 75,000 National Guardsmen in May and sent them to join the Regulars on the border. Their number was doubled in June.

Twelve days after crossing the border, the Punitive Expedition set up headquarters at Colonia Dublan near the Casas Grandes River, 125 miles south of Columbus in the Mexican state of Chihuahua. Up to that point, Villa had stayed close to the river, and his trail had been easy to follow, but here he split up his army into several units. Pershing sent swift columns of the 7th, 10th, 11th and 13th Cavalry south into the desert and mountain vastness with orders to find Villa and bring him back dead or alive. Cut off from any base, these columns had to live off the land in the way of the old cavalry of the Indian wars: it was, in fact, the last campaign of the old US Cavalry. Each horse carried about 250 pounds through the heat, wind and dust of the Chihuahua desert, shivering at night in the high-altitude cold. Quite likely, Villa's forces hid in the little towns the expedition was forbidden to enter. During his first press conference, held at Colonia Dublan, when asked how long it would take to get Villa, one of Pershing's scouts replied that they had Villa completely surrounded – on one side. The General said the campaign might be just beginning.

161

On 29 March, at seven o'clock in the morning, after a 17-hour march through freezing weather over a precipitous mountain range, 400 horsemen of Colonel George A Dodd's 7th Cavalry made contact with Villa and 500 of his men at Guerrero, west of Chihuahua City. This would be the only battle of the expedition directly involving the rebel leader. The *Villistas* fired first, and the 7th Cavalry responded, killing 60 – including the commanding officer – and wounding many others before the Mexicans fled. Dodd followed Villa until his army evaporated into cities and areas the expedition was forbidden to enter. Dodd was certain he could have cut off escape routes and taken Villa if he had arrived at Guerrero a few hours earlier.

Pershing had now penetrated 270 miles south of Columbus, and learned that Crook's methods of using local informants and native scouts in the Indian wars would not work in Mexico. Mexicans of all tribes and castes considered Villa and his Yaquis patriots, and sheltered them from the invading *norteamericanos*; informants often led the troopers on circuitous routes that gave the *Villistas* plenty of time to escape. Nevertheless, on 10 April Major Frank Tompkins with two troops of the 13th Cavalry trailed Villa into the city of Parral, about 150 miles south of Chihuahua City. At Parral he was invited in by the *Carranzista* General Ismael Lozano to refresh himself and his troops. Smelling a trap, Tompkins got his men out of town quickly under the leveled guns of the *Carranzista* garrison. Once outside the city where he had been advised to camp, he was attacked by a superior force of *Carranzistas* who pursued him for 15 miles and forced him to retreat north. On the journey his rearguard killed at least 40 of their attackers. There was no longer any question that the whole countryside opposed the invading *gringos*. Pershing asked for and got more troops, but even with civilian truck convoys beginning to work, without trains it was nearly impossible to supply them. Villa broke his command into small bands and scattered them all over the country. Pershing did the same, organizing his command into five separate and autonomous districts, despairing of receiving any accurate information from native informants: 'I have the honor to inform you that according to all information that is true and verified, Villa is at this moment in all parts and none in particular.'

Even so, the cavalry continued to engage roving bands of *Villistas*, and Major Robert L Howze devastated the bands of two of Villa's lieutenants, Acosta and Dominguez. By June there were US Army troops all over Mexico. News reached Pershing that Villa had been killed in a battle with *Carranzistas*; American intelligence concluded that Carranza was determined to force Pershing's expedition out of Mexico. Carranza himself said Villa was dead, and that the *Yanquis* had no more business in Mexico. Other rumors claimed that Villa was armed by Germany. With Mexican troops reported moving into the Parral area, Pershing requested another cavalry regiment, and expansion of all units to maximum strength. But a rumor reached Washington that Germany was backing Carranza, and that he had agreed to move his army between Pershing and the border to prevent the US Regular Army from participating in the war in Europe.

Left: *General John J Pershing (left) with staff members of the 10th Cavalry during the Punitive Expedition into Mexico in 1916.*

Right: *Pershing's pursuit of Pancho Villa in 1916 was hamstrung by numerous restrictions placed upon him by President Woodrow Wilson. At the time, Wilson was more concerned about the protracted war in Europe than about the Mexican Revolution.*

In June, when hope of catching Villa had been effectively abandoned, Carranza's commander of the North advised Pershing to go home, informing him that Mexico would not permit him to move American soldiers west, south, or east. Shortly thereafter, at a time when Pershing had already consolidated his forces at Colonia Dublan – and the principal activity of the cavalry had become polo – a large force of *Carranzistas* opened fire on two troops of the 10th Cavalry whose commander foolishly led them through the town of Carrizal. Two officers and ten men were killed, 11 wounded, and 23 troopers taken prisoner. At this point President Wilson called in most of the remaining National Guardsmen to police the border, and war probably would have broken out then and there but for the bitter struggle raging in Europe. Anxious not to become embroiled in a war with Mexico at a time when war with Germany was a growing possibility, Wilson agreed to submit the disputes stemming from the expedition to a joint commission for settlement. In January 1917, as relations between the United States and Germany reached the critical stage, the expedition was withdrawn. The last unit of the last cavalry expedition of the US Cavalry crossed the border at 3:00 PM on Monday, 5 February 1917.

Although Pershing failed to capture Villa, he probably would have if the *Carranzistas* had cooperated, or if the cavalry had been allowed a free hand. In any case, both Villa and Carranza were assassinated within the next year. The dispersal of Villa's band and the strengthening of border forces put an end to serious border incidents. More important, from a military point of view, not since the Civil War had a sizable

Top: *US Cavalry training remained much the same as it had been in the nineteenth century almost until World War II.*

Above: *Saber practice combined with jumping.*

Opposite: *Both horse and rider seem doubtful that they can negotiate the steep incline successfully in this equestrian-training photo from the early 1920s.*

Picture Credits
American Graphic Systems: 32–3 (below), 33, 131, 132 (left), 137 (top right & below), 142 (right).
Bibliothèque Nationale, Paris: 10 (bottom), 11 (bottom).
Bison Picture Library: 26 (top), 67 (below), 79 (both), 161, 171 (below).
Bodleian Library, Oxford: 11 (top, center), 12 (below, both).
British Museum Library Board: 10 (center), 11 (left & top right).
Anne S K Brown Military Collection, Brown University Library: 30 (top), 31 (both), 35 (above), 36 (above), 38-9 (all), 49 (below), 64, 65 (below), 66-7 (above), 66 (below), 70-71, 72-3, 74-5, 114-15, 118 (all), 119 (both), 126-7 (above), 148-9.
California State Library: 48-9.
Chicago Historical Society: 15.
Colorado Historical Society: 122.
Corcoran Gallery of Art, Washington, DC: 45 (below).
Currier and Ives: 78 (top).
Mary Evans Picture Library: 9 (below).
Harper's Weekly: 92 (above).
Imperial War Museum, London: 180 (center).
H W Koch Collection: 9 (above).
Eric Lessing: 10 (top).
Library of Congress: 14 (below), 16-17, 20, 24-5, 37 (below), 46 (below), 48 (left), 52 (top), 54-5, 57 (below), 58-9 (both), 60-61 (above), 61 (below), 62 (both), 63, 67 (above), 68, 68-9 (above), 69 , 70 (left), 73 (below), 82-3, 84, 86

(top), 87, 88-9, 90 (left), 90-91, 94-5, 97, 98-9 (above), 100, 101 (above), 102-03, 104-05 (above), 105, 107 (above), 108, 110-11, 112-13 (all), 116 (right), 125 (above), 128 (below), 129 (below), 132-3, 138, 140-41 (below), 142 (left), 143 (both), 150 (above), 151 (above), 153 (above), 155 (left, both), 157, 162-3, 164 (top), 165, 168, 169 (top), 174, 175 (both).
Metropolitan Museum of Art, New York, New York: 17 (right).
Elizabeth Myles Montgomery: 129 (top).
Museum of the City of New York: 27.
National Archives: 29 (below), 44-5 (above), 117 (inset), 120-21, 124 (above), 125 (below), 128 (above), 130, 134 (both), 136 (left), 136-7, 141 (top), 144-5 (both), 152-3 (main picture), 158, 159 (below), 161 (top).
National Museum of American Art: 26 (below).
National Portrait Gallery, Smithsonian Institution; on loan from the National Museum of American Art: 26 (below).
National Museum of American Art, Smithsonian Institution: 44 (below).
Peter Newark's Historical Pictures: 8, 12 (top), 13 (left, both), 21 (both), 28 (below), 65 (top), 76 (both), 77.
Peter Newark's Western Americana: 13 (right), 16 (left), 19 (below), 23 (below), 32-3 (above), 34, 34-5, 36, 37 (above), 42, 43 (both), 46 (above), 46-7, 52 (below), 53, 56 (left), 56-7, 60 (below), 80 (all), 85 (both), 92-3, 96 (both), 99 (below), 101 (below), 104 (below), 107 (below), 109 (both), 117 (main picture), 123 (both), 124

(below), 126 (left, both), 126-7 (below), 127 (right, both), 140 (top), 146-7 (main picture), 151 (below), 152 (above), 155 (top right), 160, 162 (left), 170, 173 (top), 180 (top).
The New York Historical Society, New York City: 28-9, 30 (below left).
New York Public Library Picture Collection: 14 (top), 18, 19 (above), 81.
Smithsonian Institution, National Anthropological Archives: 133 (below), 135, 139 (below), 144 (below), 146 (left).
South Dakota State Historical Society: 139 (top), 147 (inset).
US Army Photo: 169 (below), 171 (top), 176 (both), 178 (both), 178-9.
US Cavalry Museum, Fort Riley, Kansas: 150 (below), 164 (below), 172 (top), 172-3.
US Defense Department: 41 (inset), 166-7, 177 (both), 178-9 (inset), 179 (top), 181 (both), 183 (top), 185 (top), 185 (below right), 188-9.
US Navy, Naval Photographic Center: 40-41, 86 (below), 106, 154, 156 (left), 156 (right), 159 (top).
Valley Forge Historical Society: 6-7.
Yale University Art Gallery, Joseph Szaszfai photo: 22-3.

Acknowledgments
The publisher would like to thank the following people who have helped in the preparation of this book: Michael Rose, who designed it; Robin Langley Sommer, who edited it; Mary R Raho, who did the picture research; and Florence Norton, who prepared the index.